Pamphlet Series

The System of Macroeconomic Accounts Statistics

An Overview

Statistics Department
INTERNATIONAL MONETARY FUND
Washington, D.C.
2007

ISBN 978-1-58906-620-5
ISSN 0538-8759
August 2007

The views expressed in this pamphlet, including any legal aspects, are those of the author and should not be attributed to Executive Directors of the IMF or their national authorities.

Cover design and typesetting: Multimedia Services Division

Please send orders to:
International Monetary Fund, Publication Services
700 19th Street, N.W., Washington, D.C. 20431, USA
Tel.: (202) 623-7430   Telefax: (202) 623-7201
E-mail: publications@imf.org
Internet: http://www.imf.org

Contents

The following conventions are used in this publication:

- In tables, a blank cell indicates "not applicable," ellipsis points (. . .) indicate "not available," and 0 or 0.0 indicates "zero" or "negligible." Minor discrepancies between sums of constituent figures and totals are due to rounding.
- An en dash (–) between years or months (for example, 1998–99 or January–June) indicates the years or months covered, including the beginning and ending years or months; a slash or virgule (/) between years or months (for example, 1998/99) indicates a fiscal or financial year, as does the abbreviation FY (for example, FY2006).
- "Billion" means a thousand million; "trillion" means a thousand billion.
- "Basis points" refer to hundredths of 1 percentage point (for example, 25 basis points are equivalent to 1/4 of 1 percentage point).

As used in this publication, the term "country" does not in all cases refer to a territorial entity that is a state as understood by international law and practice. As used here, the term also covers some territorial entities that are not states but for which statistical data are maintained on a separate and independent basis.

Foreword

Designed to meet the needs of economists, statisticians, students, and others, this pamphlet broadly surveys the key principles underlying the four main sets of macroeconomic statistics—national accounts, balance of payments, monetary and financial, and government finance statistics—when viewed as an integrated system. In this respect, it highlights the relationships between sectors of statistics and discusses recent developments in statistical methodologies, data compilation, and policy analysis and evaluation. The pamphlet updates *Macroeconomic Accounts: An Overview*, published by the IMF in 1979 under the authorship of Poul Høst-Madsen.

Manuals and guidelines on statistical frameworks are available for the four main areas of macroeconomic statistics, but the reader can easily be overwhelmed by the very size of the manuals and their technical content. Moreover, understanding the relationship between these statistics through the existing manuals can be challenging for specialists and nonspecialists alike. Thus, this pamphlet bridges the various statistics, simplifying many concepts for purposes of exposition, to help the reader to understand the main relationships underlying the sets of macroeconomic statistics. In showing how the four key statistical areas harmonize, the pamphlet explains their common features and differences. It also provides numerical examples in each chapter to demonstrate the practical application and uses of the concepts within an analytical framework.

In demonstrating the mutual consistency of the macroeconomic statistics, the pamphlet serves the needs of both policymakers and students of statistics. Given the orientation of the pamphlet, the authors expect it to be a valuable resource for students of economics and statistics to learn about macroeconomic statistics. At the same time, it should serve as a tool for IMF staff training, as well as for the IMF's external training. Of course, for specialists or students wishing to have more in-depth understanding of the international concepts and frameworks in each macroeconomic account, they may refer to the relevant statistical manuals or guides.

Preparing the pamphlet has been a long and complex endeavor involving numerous specialists with diverse skills who were able to build on each other's work through the exchange of drafts and consultations. The project was managed under a task force headed by Neil Patterson (former Assistant Director of the Statistics Department) that comprised Edgar Ayales, Keith Dublin, Roberto Rosales, Robin Kibuka, Wipada Soonthornsima, and Emmanuel Kumah. The task force reviewed the main draft chapters of the pamphlet prepared by Statistics Department consultants Paul Cotterell and Kevin O'Connor.

Besides preparing additional materials for the pamphlet, the task force requested and received supplementary materials from other Statistics Department staff, including, in particular, Kim Zieschang, Cor Gorter, Mick Silver, and Jose Cartas. The pamphlet benefited from useful comments from many staff of the Statistics Department. Further, particular note should be made of the contributions and inputs from other IMF departments that have strengthened and enriched the pamphlet in terms of its policy and practical content. Carmen Diaz-Zelaya and Patricia Poggi provided secretarial assistance; Joan Gibson gave editorial assistance; and James McEuen of the External Relations Department coordinated copyediting and publication. I wish to thank all who have contributed to this pamphlet.

Robert W. Edwards
Director
Statistics Department
International Monetary Fund

Abbreviations

BPM5	*Balance of Payments Manual, fifth edition*
BSA	Balance sheet approach
COFOG	Classification of the Functions of Government
CPI	Consumer price index
CPIS	Coordinated Portfolio Investment Survey (IMF)
DCS	Depository corporations survey
DQAF	Data Quality Assessment Framework
FCS	Financial corporations survey
FISIM	Financial intermediation services indirectly measured
f.o.b.	Free on board
FP	Financial programming
FSI	Financial soundness indicator
GDDS	General Data Dissemination System
GDI	Gross domestic income
GDP	Gross domestic product
GDY	Gross national disposable income
GFS	Government finance statistics
GFSM 1986	*A Manual on Government Finance Statistics 1986*
GFSM 2001	*Government Finance Statistics Manual 2001*
GNI	Gross national income
GNP	Gross national product
IIP	International investment position
ILO	International Labor Organization
IMF	International Monetary Fund
ITS	International trade in services
MA	Monetary aggregate
MFP	Multifactor productivity
MFSM	*Monetary and Financial Statistics Manual*
n.i.e.	Not indicated elsewhere
NL/B	Net lending/borrowing
NOB	Net operating balance
NPI	Nonprofit institution
NPISH	Nonprofit institutions serving households
OECD	Organization for Economic Cooperation and Development

PPI	Producer price index
QNA	Quarterly national accounts
ROSC	Report on the Observance of Standards and Codes
SDDS	Special Data Dissemination Standard (IMF)
SDR	Special drawing right
SEEA	System of Environmental and Economic Accounting (UN)
1993 SNA	*System of National Accounts 1993*
SUT	Supply and use table
UN	United Nations
XMPI	Export and import price index

I

Introduction

Aimed primarily at meeting the needs of economists and statisticians, this pamphlet concisely describes the principles underlying the four main sets of macroeconomic accounts statistics, viewed as an integrated system. The four main sets are the national accounts, balance of payments and international investment position, monetary and financial statistics, and government finance statistics. To illustrate the relationships among the sets, the pamphlet covers statistics on transactions, stock data (asset and liability positions), and the linkages between stock data and transactions, as well as some economic statistical series closely related to these accounts.

This pamphlet also takes account of new developments in standards for macroeconomic statistics. The standards for preparing statistics in the four main areas were revised following the publication of the *System of National Accounts 1993* (*1993 SNA*),[1] which set out the overarching conceptual framework for all macroeconomic statistics. The *1993 SNA* incorporated two significant enhancements: the full integration of stocks (balance sheets) and flows, and a complete sets of accounts covering production, income, consumption, saving, investment, and financial activities for sectors of the economy as well as for the economy as a whole.

Coincident with the publication of the *1993 SNA*, the IMF revised the methodology for balance of payments statistics—also broadening its scope to include the international investment position—and published the *Balance of Payments Manual,* fifth edition (*BPM5*; IMF, 1993), also in 1993. Subsequently, the IMF developed the methodology for monetary and financial statistics—published as the *Monetary and Financial Statistics Manual* (*MFSM*; IMF, 2000c)—and revised the methodology for government finance statistics—published as the *Government Finance Statistics Manual 2001* (*GFSM 2001*; IMF, 2001).

---

[1]Published jointly: Commission of the European Communities—Eurostat, IMF, Organization for Economic Cooperation and Development (OECD), United Nations (UN), and World Bank (1993).

Developed by the IMF in close consultation with country experts and other international agencies, each statistical standard has been recognized as the international standard for the sector. Although the standards have been harmonized with the *1993 SNA*, each is also oriented toward important policy variables not covered by the national accounts, such as measures of the balance of payments surplus or deficit, the fiscal position, and money and credit measures. At the time of this writing, the *1993 SNA* and the *BPM5* are again being updated in harmony to take account of new developments in economic activities and analysis since 1993.[2]

Standards for macroeconomic statistics are thus not lacking, but the reader can easily be overwhelmed by the very size of the various manuals and sometimes by the language in them. Thus, for purposes of broad exposition of the meaning and uses of macroeconomic statistics, this pamphlet simplifies many concepts. For an understanding of the standards in detail, readers should refer to the relevant statistical manuals or guides.

An important feature of the sets of macroeconomic statistics is the use of the same basic concepts. Thus, before the pamphlet addresses each main macroeconomic account, this introduction describes the features in common. It then concludes with sections on data quality and the practical applications of the *1993 SNA* framework.

Common Features of Macroeconomic Statistics

Macroeconomic statistics are aimed at one broad purpose—to serve decision makers—and this purpose can best be accomplished if the statistics are, as far as practicable, mutually consistent. It was with this objective in mind that the IMF revised and harmonized the manuals for the balance of payments, government finance, and monetary statistics with the *1993 SNA*.

This section discusses common features of macroeconomic statistics: institutional units and sectors; residence; stocks (assets/liabilities), economic flows, and their integration; accounting rules; and market price valuation and conversion procedures.

---

[2]This pamphlet is based on the current international standards, but see http://unstats.un.org/unsd/nationalaccount/iswgna.htm and http://www.imf.org/external/np/sta/bop/bopman5.htm for information about their review.

Institutional Units and Sectors

The basic building block of macroeconomic statistics is the *institutional unit*. This section describes the two types of units and the five sectors into which these units are grouped.

Units

National data compilers obtain and combine as statistics the information on economic activities of the institutional unit. An institutional unit is defined as *an economic entity capable, in its own right, of owning assets, incurring liabilities, and engaging in other economic activities and transactions with other entities.* In other words, an institutional unit is an entity that can act economically on its own behalf and be held directly responsible and accountable for those actions. In particular, on its own behalf, it is able to own assets and incur liabilities. For the unit, data compilers could find a complete set of accounts existing (including a balance sheet), or they would find it possible and meaningful to compile a complete set of accounts for it.

Two main types of entities qualify as institutional units—*households* and *legal and social entities* whose existence is recognized independently of the persons, or other entities, that may own or control them.

In the first type, individual members of multiperson households are not treated as separate institutional units because they own many assets jointly, incur liabilities jointly, often pool income, and decide collectively about expenditures for the household as a whole.

The second type of unit comprises corporations, government units, and nonprofit institutions. *Corporations* produce goods and services for the market and may be a source of profit to their owners, whereas *government units* primarily produce goods and services on a nonmarket basis. *Nonprofit institutions* (NPIs) may be market or nonmarket producers but cannot be a source of profit to their owners.[3] In much the same way as corporations, some unincorporated entities belonging to households or government units may produce market goods and services. If they have a complete set of accounts, or if it is possible and

---

[3]Market producers sell most or all of their output at economically significant prices (that is, at prices that have a significant influence on the amount producers are willing to supply or on the amounts purchasers wish to purchase). Nonmarket producers provide most or all of their output to others free or at prices that are not economically significant.

3

meaningful to compile a complete set of accounts, statisticians consider them to be quasi-corporations and treat them as corporations.

Sectors

Institutional units are grouped into five mutually exclusive institutional *sectors* of the economy according to their different economic objectives, functions, and behavior. The sectors are

- Nonfinancial corporations sector,
- Financial corporations sector,
- General government sector,
- Nonprofit institutions serving households (NPISH) sector, and
- Household sector.

Among the five, the two sectors of corporations comprise not only corporations but also quasi-corporations and NPIs that are market producers. The general government sector comprises general government units that are not treated as quasi-corporations and nonmarket NPIs that are controlled and mainly financed by government units. The NPISH sector comprises nonmarket NPIs not controlled by government. Finally, the household sector comprises households and their unincorporated enterprises that are not treated as quasi-corporations.

Residence

All macroeconomic statistics relate to an economy—defined to comprise all its resident institutional units. This section defines (1) *resident*, (2) *nonresident*, (3) *economic territory*, and (4) *economic interest*; it also discusses how institutional sectors relate to residence.

Residents designates institutional units that have a closer tie with the economic territory of the country in question than with any other country. Residence is not based on nationality or currency of denomination; rather, it is based on where the unit's center of economic interest lies.

As for *nonresidents*, units that are not residents of the given economy are residents of the rest of the world and are termed nonresidents.

The *economic territory* of a country consists of the geographic territory administered by a government. Within the territory, persons, goods, and capital circulate freely. It includes airspace, territorial waters, and continental shelf lying in international waters over which the country enjoys exclusive rights or over which it has, or claims to have, jurisdiction with respect to economic exploitation. It also includes territorial enclaves in the rest of the world, such as embassies, consulates, and military bases.

Regarding *economic interest,* an institutional unit has a center of economic interest within a country when there exists some location—dwelling, place of production, or other premises—within the economic territory of the country from which the unit engages in economic activities significantly, either indefinitely or over a finite but long period. Normally, a one-year rule is applied.

How do the institutional sectors relate to residence?

In relation to the *general government sector,* a country's general government units at all levels (central, state, local) are regarded as resident of that country—that is, part of the domestic economy—even when they carry out activities abroad. Thus, any embassies, consulates, military bases, and other general government units located abroad are treated as residents of the home country, as are its nationals assigned to such agencies. Conversely, the embassies, consulates, and so forth maintained by a foreign government in a given country are nonresidents, as are their personnel who are not recruited locally. Similarly, international organizations whose members are governments are treated as nonresidents of the country in which they are located. However, the residency of the staff of an international organization is determined according to the criteria applied to other households in the country.

Regarding the *two corporate sectors*, a corporation (public or private) is a resident of a country (economic territory) when it is engaged in a significant amount of production there or when it owns land or buildings there, even when the corporation is owned wholly or partly by nonresidents. A branch or subsidiary of a foreign corporation located in a given country, therefore, is regarded as a resident of that country. Conversely, the foreign branches and subsidiaries of resident corporations are regarded as nonresidents. Offshore enterprises are residents of the economy in which the offshore enterprise is located, regardless of whether they are in special zones of exemption from customs or other regulations.

Regarding the *household sector*, household units may be more difficult to classify as resident or nonresident. A household has residency in a country when it maintains a dwelling in that country that is used by members of the household as their principal residence. Therefore, those who live permanently in a country are regarded as residents, even when they are temporarily abroad—for example as tourists or as business travelers. Similarly, individuals who work abroad but return to the household after a limited period (for example, seasonal workers and border workers) are treated as residents of the economy in which they maintain their household, even if they make frequent journeys abroad over a long period.

Conversely, also regarding households, an individual normally ceases to be a member of a resident household when he or she works abroad continuously for one year or more. The individual is deemed to have changed household, because most of the individual's consumption takes place in the country where he or she lives or works, and the individual is considered to have a center of economic interest there. Students are treated as residents of their country of origin regardless of how long they study abroad, provided they remain members of households in their home countries.

Stocks, Flows, and Their Integration

Stocks

Stocks, another common feature of the macroeconomic statistics, are economic magnitudes *measured at a point in time*. That is, they are positions in, or holdings of, *assets* and *liabilities* at a point in time. Assets must be owned by an institutional unit and can be expected to provide economic benefit to the owner. The economic benefit may arise through the use of the asset in production (for example, a machine or building) or the generation of income by the asset (interest, dividends, or rent) or the holding of the asset as a store of value.

Stocks are recorded in the *balance sheet* (Box 1) at the beginning and end of the accounting period. Stocks are to be valued at current market prices on the day the balance sheet is drawn up.

Looking further at assets (either nonfinancial or financial) and liabilities, this section provides examples of financial assets and illustrates the difference between a unit's total stock of assets and its stock of liabilities—net worth.

Assets, within the systems of macroeconomic statistics, are defined as entities over which institutional units—individually or collectively— enforce ownership rights and from which they can derive economic benefits by holding or using the assets over a period.

Assets are either *nonfinancial* (such as land, machinery and equipment, and inventories) or *financial* (generally representing claims of one unit on another), whereas *liabilities* are financial obligations of one unit to another and are, therefore, the counterpart to financial assets.

6

Nonfinancial assets include produced assets, such as machinery and equipment, and nonproduced assets, such as land, and also include intangible assets, such as computer software.

Most *financial assets* involve claims arising from one institutional unit that is providing resources to another unit that must be repaid. The unit providing the resources has a claim (asset), and the unit that must repay has a liability, displaying an asset/liability symmetry.

Typical examples of financial assets/liabilities are currency (an asset for the holder and a liability for the central bank); deposits (an asset for the depositor and a liability for the bank); and loans (an asset for the lender and a liability for the borrower). Securities display the financial asset/liability symmetry as well. Financial assets also include the ownership of corporations in the form of shares issued by the corporation. The shares are considered to be financial claims of the owners and liabilities of the corporation.

Further examples of financial assets are monetary gold and SDRs (special drawing rights, the IMF's unit of account), considered assets by convention and used by monetary authorities to settle international payments, although they do not reflect claims on other designated units. Monetary gold consists only of gold held by the central bank or government as part of official reserves. SDRs are international reserve assets created by the IMF and allocated to members to supplement existing official reserves.

Not to be considered as financial assets are some financial contracts, such as guarantees, letters of credit, and loan commitments (conditional on some future event occurring). However, on these contracts, data compilers often find it useful to collect information, because contracts can indicate possible future risks for the units with the commitments.

A detailed discussion of the list of financial assets and liabilities (financial instruments) can be found in Box 2.

The difference between a unit's total stock of assets (financial and nonfinancial) and its stock of liabilities is defined as *net worth*. When measuring net worth, analysts include a corporation's shares and other equity obligations in its stock of liabilities. Therefore, net worth is a different concept from net equity and shareholders' funds used in commercial accounting.

Flows

Compared with stocks, *flows* are economic magnitudes *measured with reference to a period of time*, and they have two types—*transactions*

Box 1. Balance Sheet

Balance sheets are statements, drawn up at a particular point, showing the values of all assets owned by an institutional unit and the values of all the liabilities of that unit. In the T-account presentation, assets are recorded on the left-hand side of the balance sheet and liabilities on the right. The difference between the total stock of assets and the total stock of liabilities is the *net worth* of the unit, which is also recorded on the right-hand side of the balance sheet, whether it is positive or negative. Balance sheets for sectors of the economy and the economy as a whole can be compiled from the data on individual units.

Net worth as measured in the macroeconomic accounts should not be confused with *net equity* (total assets minus total liabilities) as measured in commercial accounting, where liabilities exclude the value of shares and other equity. In the macroeconomic accounts, the stake of shareholders in a corporation is measured through shares and other equity and is included as a liability. Because net worth excludes all liabilities, including the value of shares and other equity, a corporation can have a net worth of its own that is separate from the aggregate stake of the shareholders.

The stock of assets and liabilities recorded in the balance sheet is to be valued at *market prices*. Sometimes, direct observations are available—such as in prices fetched on the stock exchange. When no direct observations are available, market prices for close substitutes may be used. For fixed assets, balance sheet values are often estimated using a perpetual inventory method, whereby information on acquisitions over many years is accumulated, revalued using appropriate price indices, and amortized using rates based on the expected life of the assets involved. In the case of assets whose returns are spread over a long period, the estimation of net present value of the future returns may be used. The valuation of financial items should include any accrued interest.

Readers should note that the *closing balance sheet* of one period is identical to the opening balance sheet of the next period. Also, the changes in the holding of assets and liabilities that occur during an accounting period can be fully explained by either transactions or other economic flows (revaluations and other volume changes). In other words, for each asset and liability, the closing balance sheet value is equal to the opening balance sheet value plus transactions plus other economic flows. This identity provides a very useful compilation and analytic tool.

(further delineated into exchanges or transfers) and *other economic flows* (further delineated into holding gains and losses and changes in the volume of the asset). Flows fully reflect the change in the value of the stock

The existence of a *set of balance sheets* integrated with the flow accounts enables analysts to verify the reasonableness of the statistics by analyzing the components of the change in the balance sheet from one period to the next. It also allows analysts to look more broadly in monitoring and assessing economic conditions and behavior. For example, in determining household behavior, analysts can use wealth variables in consumption and savings functions to capture the impact of these functions; that is, they capture the effects of other flows in assets (such as price fluctuations) and the impact these have on households' purchasing patterns. Analysts also need household balance sheets to assess the distribution of wealth and liquidity.

Balance sheet data on the level and composition of *tangible, intangible,* and *financial assets* are of considerable interest for indicating the economic resources of a nation and for assessing the external debtor or creditor position of a country. Interested parties can analyze changes in the structure of assets and liabilities using balance sheets for different periods—for example, to assess whether infrastructure assets are being adequately maintained or whether the portfolio of financial assets (or debt liabilities) is appropriate. Such information may not be apparent from transactions data and requires details of the stocks of assets and liabilities involved.

Balance sheets in business accounting are likely to differ from the macroeconomic accounts balance sheets in the following ways:
- Enterprises often value items at historic cost rather than current market prices.
- The value of fixed capital in enterprise accounts is usually influenced by tax rules on depreciation allowances.
- Similarly, shares are sometimes valued at nominal or issue prices rather than current market prices.
- Enterprise balance sheets include provisions for contingent risk that are not included as liabilities in macroeconomic accounts.

Therefore, analysts need to adjust balance sheet data of business accounts before including them in the balance sheet accounts of macroeconomic accounts. For instance, it would be problematic to combine the historic-cost balance sheets of individual units to provide sectoral or economy-wide balance sheets because the valuations used for the assets and liabilities involved would not be consistent.

of an asset or liability during the accounting period. Compilers measure the two types of flows at market prices at the time the transaction or other economic flow takes place.

Box 2. Financial Assets and Liabilities

All the statistical systems recognize eight categories of financial assets (with or without corresponding liabilities).

- *Monetary gold and SDRs* are financial assets by convention, because monetary authorities may use them in settling financial claims. Monetary gold is a financial asset not having a corresponding liability. SDR holdings are treated as financial assets because they represent unconditional rights to obtain foreign exchange or other reserve assets from other IMF members. IMF member countries to which SDRs are allocated are not regarded as having an actual (unconditional) liability to repay their SDR allocations. However, the allocations resemble liabilities, and many IMF member countries show a liability entry in their accounts equal to their original SDR allocations.
- *Currency and deposits* comprise the most liquid financial assets. Currency consists of notes and coins of fixed nominal value and generally usable directly for transactions. Currency is issued by central banks and governments. Deposits fall into two broad types—transferable and other deposits (savings, time, fixed). Transferable deposits are exchangeable at par on demand and can be used directly for transactions. Other deposits have some forms of restriction but are often very easily converted into transferable deposits and are therefore close substitutes.
- *Securities other than shares* are negotiable instruments that serve as evidence of a unit's obligations, most often to pay interest and to repay a principal amount at maturity. Securities other than shares may pay a specific amount of interest or may sell at a discount with interest calculated as the difference between the face value and the sale price. Short-term securities, particularly those issued by depository corporations, may be very close substitutes for deposits.

Transactions are interactions among institutional units by mutual agreement.[4] They may be of two kinds—*exchanges* or *transfers*.

The first kind of transaction, an *exchange,* involves one party providing a good, service, labor, or asset to another party and receiving a counterpart in return. For example, a unit may exchange goods and services for a

---

[4]Transactions also include some activities internal to a unit that are analytically useful to treat as being between two units. For example, consumption of fixed capital is treated as a transaction even though only one unit is involved. Each of the statistical systems regards the unit as acting in two capacities—as the user of the fixed asset and the owner of the asset.

- *Loans* are financial claims created when a creditor provides funds directly to a debtor, and the resulting claim is nonnegotiable. Loans generally pay interest that may be fixed or adjustable to changes in a contractually agreed base. Loans may become negotiable, and, in that case, they should be reclassified as securities.
- *Shares and other equities* are evidence of ownership of a corporation that gives to the owner claims on the residual value of the corporation after creditors' claims have been met. Shares and other equity may pay property income in the form of dividends and may be held with the expectation of achieving holding gains.
- *Insurance technical reserves* are the liabilities of insurance companies and pension funds to participants. These liabilities include net equity of households in life insurance reserves, net equity of households in pension funds, amounts outstanding but not earned when premiums are prepaid, and amounts reserved for outstanding claims.
- *Financial derivatives* are instruments linked to a specific financial instrument, indicator, or commodity. Through them, specific financial risks (such as interest rate risk; currency, equity, and commodity price risk; credit risk; and so forth) can be traded in their own right in financial markets. The value of a derivative instrument derives from the price of the underlying item such as an asset or index. The two broad types of financial derivatives are forward-type contracts and option contracts.
- *Other accounts receivable/payable* include trade credit and advances and a wide range of miscellaneous creditor/debtor relationships that do not fall under the other categories.

financial asset, or it may receive cash (a financial asset) in exchange for the obligation to repay the cash (a loan liability). Readers should note that in the latter case, the lender has exchanged a financial asset (the cash) for another financial asset (the loan).

The second kind, a *transfer,* involves one party providing a good, service, labor, or asset to another without receiving anything in return. An example is one government donating food and medical supplies to another in response to a natural disaster. Also considered a transfer is the payment of taxes, even though the taxpayer is able to benefit from the collective services provided by government and funded from tax revenue. This is because no direct link exists between the amount of tax payable and benefits received.

The other type of flow, *other economic flows,* is all the changes in the stock of an asset (or liability) that do not arise from transactions. The two kinds are *holding gains and losses* and *changes in the volume of the asset.*

The first kind of other economic flow, a *holding gain or loss*, arises when the market price of the asset changes during the period, including changes in the domestic value of assets denominated in a foreign currency when the exchange rate of that currency changes.

The second kind, a *change in the volume of an asset*, covers a wide variety of events, including the discovery of new natural resources, depletion of subsoil assets, destruction of assets through natural disaster, and debt write-off.

Integration of stocks and flows

It follows from the above definitions of stocks and flows that the total change in the stock of each asset or liability from the beginning of a period to the end of the period is explained fully by the flows. That is,

Stock (end) = Stock (beginning) + Transactions + Other Economic Flows.

For example, at the beginning of the period a unit has $100 in a bank account. During the period it deposits $30 and withdraws $10, giving a net increase in the bank account of $20 from transactions. If there are no other changes, the stock in the bank account at the end of the period would be $120, representing the stock at the beginning plus the net transactions.

However, the unit may also own an asset with a market price that changes from day to day, such as shares in a corporation. In this case, even without any transactions, the value of the stock of shares is likely to differ at the end of the period from its value at the start because of price changes for the shares. This change in stock values would be recorded not as a transaction but as an other economic flow. In other cases, both transactions and other economic flows may take place during the period, and together they explain the total change in the stock.

This integration of stocks and flows provides a useful check on the accuracy of the data for both stocks and transactions by revealing information on the other economic flows. For instance, analysts could check the size of the revaluations and other volume changes to ensure they are consistent with known economic conditions. Further, because transaction data are sometimes estimated from changes in the stock data, analysts need to exercise care to ensure they or other parties have taken account of any other economic flows that may have occurred during the period.

Accounting Rules

A fourth common feature of macroeconomic statistics is *accounting rules*. All systems of macroeconomic statistics are based on the double-entry accounting system, whereby the accountants have recorded every flow twice—as a *debit entry* and as a *credit entry*. The accounting rule concept also hinges on *accrual and cash recording*.

Debits and credits

The *debit entry* refers to the increase in an asset, decrease in a liability, or decrease in net worth (for example, an expense) of the unit. The *credit entry* refers to the counterpart increase in a liability, decrease in an asset, or increase in net worth (for example, revenue) of the unit.

For example, a household may provide labor to a corporation in exchange for cash. The household unit would record this as a debit entry for the increased cash asset and a credit for its increased net worth (the wages and salaries revenue). Conversely, the corporation would record a credit for the reduction in cash and a debit for the decrease in its net worth (the wages and salaries expense).[5]

Credits include

- Sales of goods and services (including exports),
- Property income receivable,
- Compensation of employees receivable by households,
- Transfers receivable (including tax revenue for government),
- Increases in liabilities,
- Decreases in nonfinancial assets (including inventories), and
- Decreases in financial assets.

Debits include

- Purchases of goods and services (including imports),
- Property income payable,

---

[5]In the national accounts, entries would be recorded for both the household unit and the corporation, resulting in quadruple recording of the transaction.

- Compensation of employees payable by employers,
- Transfers payable,
- Decreases in liabilities,
- Increases in nonfinancial assets (including inventories), and
- Increases in financial assets.

Accrual and cash recording

Units record flows on an *accruals basis*, and/or a *cash basis*, in each macroeconomic statistical system. That is, they record them when units exchange, transform, create, transfer, or extinguish economic value, which is not necessarily when the units make payment. The accruals basis ensures consistency of recording among units and over time (as well as from country to country) and can completely cover economic events. On the other hand, a cash basis of recording records events only when cash is received or disbursed; it omits all noncash transactions (such as barter and in-kind transfers).

In many cases, under both accrual and cash recording, the timing will be the same for a transaction, such as the cash payment for the provision of a service. However, in other cases, the timing can differ considerably, such as provision of goods and services on credit or the recording of interest on discounted securities.

If units have not recorded the underlying statistics on an accrual basis, it is important that analysts adjust the statistics, on some estimated basis, to an approximate accrual basis to preserve the internal consistency of the macroeconomic accounts when they are to be fully integrated. Most notably, they may need to adjust for government finance statistics that were compiled on the cash-based system recommended in the earlier publication, *A Manual on Government Finance Statistics 1986* (*GFSM 1986*; IMF, 1986), particularly if significant arrears or borrowing using discounted securities exist.

Market Price Valuation and Conversion Procedures

Finally, another common feature of macroeconomic statistics sets is valuation and conversion procedure. In principle, units should measure all transactions and position (stock) data on the basis of *market prices*. This means they value transactions at the actual price agreed upon by the parties (in other words, amounts of money that willing buyers pay to acquire something from willing sellers). At the same time, they value the stock of assets and liabilities on the basis of the market prices in force at the time to which the balance sheet relates.

However, units cannot always implement the market price principle. Therefore, the staff who record macroeconomic data may find it necessary to resort to alternative measures or proxies in cases where no actual market prices have been set.

Compiling macroeconomic accounts is also complicated because, initially, units may express the transactions or stocks of assets and liabilities in different currencies. To convert these currencies into the unit of account (normally the domestic currency) adopted for compiling these statements, compilers use the most appropriate exchange rates for conversion purposes—those rates prevailing on the transaction date or those prevailing on the reporting date for valuation of stocks. A rule of thumb recommends the midpoint between buying and selling rates.

This introduction concludes by discussing data quality and the use and practical application of macroeconomic statistics.

Data Quality

Statisticians and economists always have understood the importance of providing or using high-quality statistics. In recent years, international experts have developed formal frameworks to systematically assess data quality by comparing country statistical practices with best practices, including internationally accepted conceptual standards and timely dissemination. One such framework is the IMF's Data Quality Assessment Framework (DQAF; Box 3), which was introduced in 2001 and updated in 2003 (IMF, 2003).

Use and Practical Application of Macroeconomic Statistics

Macroeconomic statistics are essential for evaluating a country's economic performance and for making cross-country and multilateral comparisons. They also provide the framework for planning, formulating, and monitoring the implementation of economic and budgetary policy. Further, they serve the needs of market participants through providing timely and transparent information.

Two examples of the use of the integrated macroeconomic accounts in the IMF's surveillance activities are the *financial programming* (FP)

Box 3. Data Quality Assessment Framework

The Data Quality Assessment Framework (DQAF; IMF, 2003) brings together a structure and common language for best practices and internationally accepted concepts and definitions in statistics, including those of the United Nations' *Fundamental Principles of Official Statistics* (UN, 1994) and the IMF's Special Data Dissemination Standard (SDDS; IMF, 2007a) and the General Data Dissemination System (GDDS; IMF, 2007b). The DQAF identifies quality-related features of governance of statistical systems, statistical processes, and statistical products. The DQAF is organized around a set of prerequisites and five dimensions of data quality—assurance of integrity, methodological soundness, accuracy and reliability, serviceability, and accessibility. The generic DQAF serves as the umbrella for the specific frameworks for the data sets. The IMF has developed the DQAF for seven macroeconomic data sets: national accounts, consumer price index, producer price index, external debt, government finance, monetary, and balance of payments.

The DQAF has proven to be valuable to at least three groups of users. First, it has guided the IMF staff on using data in policy evaluation, preparing the data module of Reports on the Observance of Standards and Codes (ROSCs), and designing technical assistance. Second, it has guided country efforts to evaluate shortcomings in the compilation of statistics, including in preparing self-assessments. Third, it has guided data users in evaluating data for policy analysis, forecasts, and economic performance.

exercise and, more recently, the *balance sheet approach* (BSA) to macroeconomic analysis.

Under the FP exercises, analysts evaluate the linkages between the main macroeconomic accounts of an economy to assess the impact of exogenous shocks and to formulate appropriate policy responses to achieve specified goals (stabilization, growth, and so forth), including by preparing alternative prospective scenarios for the medium term.

The BSA, on the other hand, exploits information from sectoral and national balance sheets to examine the countries' vulnerabilities, including vis-à-vis nonresidents. In essence, the BSA focuses on identifying and analyzing the vulnerabilities of an economy to financial and economic shocks through the evaluation of the balance sheets of its key institutional sectors. Using this approach, analysts evaluate the (1) financial position of the economy's key institutional sectors; (2) possible mismatches in maturity, currency, and term structure of assets and liabilities; and (3) potential propagation of sectoral weaknesses owing to linkages among balance sheets of different sectors. Vulnerability indicators point to potential risks that could trigger liquidity and solvency problems at times of stress. The financial crises of the late 1990s underscored the importance of balance sheet data as critical elements for vulnerability analysis.

The following chapters address each main macroeconomic account—the national accounts, balance of payments and international investment position, monetary and financial statistics, and government finance statistics—and the linkages reflecting the common features across the systems.

II
National Accounts

Many early writers on economics, such as Adam Smith, focused on national wealth as an indicator of economic strength and performance. Later writers on economic theory, such as Keynes, Frisch, and Tinbergen, focused on economic flows. One major advance that the *System of National Accounts 1993 (1993 SNA*; Commission of the European Communities and others, 1993) made was to effectively marry these two approaches by linking in detail the accounts that present transactions and other economic flows with the balance sheets that present stocks of wealth.

The *1993 SNA* provides readers with a comprehensive and systematic framework for collecting, presenting, and analyzing macroeconomic statistics. In a sequence of accounts, the framework presents a mass of details about how an economy works and how economic agents interact. Through this system, the *1993 SNA* enables users to analyze the production and use of goods and services and to measure the gross domestic product (GDP)—the basic production concept of the *1993 SNA*. It enables users to analyze the incomes generated by that production, earned from the ownership of assets and redistributed within the economy. It also allows users to identify the capital and financial flows that take place. It provides information not only about economic activity but also about the levels of an economy's productive assets and the wealth of its inhabitants.

Further, the *1993 SNA* addresses closely related issues, including methodology for compiling price and volume indices for flows of goods and services; detailed supply and use tables (SUTs) showing how economies allocate supplies of goods and services from domestic and imported sources between intermediate or final uses (including exports); information on the ways in which analysts define and classify the items in the accounts, notably the key production and asset boundaries; and labor force indicators.

The following sections (1) summarize the sequence of *1993 SNA* accounts, provided in a diagram of the *1993 SNA* framework; (2) introduce the starting point in the framework—measuring the GDP; (3) illustrate the

18

additional wealth of information found in the details of the sequence of accounts; and (4) review issues related to the *1993 SNA*, such as volume and real income measures, quarterly national accounts data, important boundaries, labor force indicators, multifactor productivity, environmental and economic accounting, and informal sector and illegal activities.

Summary: Sequence of Accounts in the *1993 SNA* Framework

Built around a sequence of interconnected flow accounts and stocks presented in balance sheets, the main sets of accounts in the *1993 SNA* framework are the *current accounts*, the *accumulation accounts*, and the *balance sheets*. In these sets, each flow account pertains to a different type of economic activity, and each balance sheet records the value of assets and liabilities held at the beginning or end of the period.

The *current accounts* comprise the *production account*, which measures GDP, and the *income accounts,* which derive national income, national disposable income, and saving.

The *accumulation accounts* consist of the *capital account*, which records transactions in nonfinancial assets and capital transfers; the *financial account*, which records transactions in financial assets and liabilities; and the accounts for *other economic flows*, which record revaluations and other changes in the volume of assets. In the capital account, the balancing item is *net lending/borrowing* (NL/B). If an economy's saving and capital transfers exceed its net acquisition of nonfinancial assets, then it is a net lender to the rest of the world. Conversely, if its net acquisition of nonfinancial assets exceeds its saving and capital transfers, it is a net borrower from the rest of the world. In the financial account, the transactions in financial assets and liabilities reflect the NL/B.

The *balance sheets* show the stock of assets and liabilities at the beginning and end of each period and are fully integrated with the transactions and other economic flows for those assets and liabilities. The balancing item for the balance sheets is *net worth*.

How are the accounts presented in the *1993 SNA* framework? The sequence of accounts and balances can be presented for the economy as a whole and/or for different institutional sectors to show the contribution of each sector to the economy. Table 1 illustrates the framework, and more detail is shown in the description of the sequence of accounts later in this chapter.

TABLE 1. *1993 SNA* FRAMEWORK

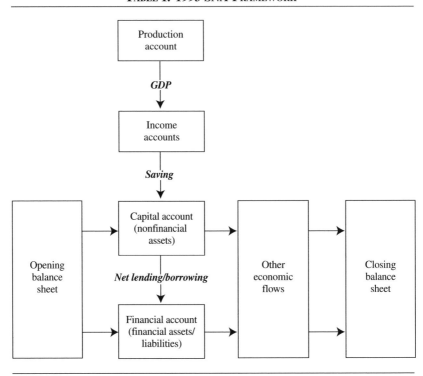

Before showing the details of the sequence of accounts, the next section illustrates the starting point of the *1993 SNA* framework—measuring the GDP, the basic production concept of the *1993 SNA*.[6]

Measuring Gross Domestic Product

To measure GDP, analysts use three standard approaches: the production, income, and expenditure approaches. In the *1993 SNA* framework, the production approach is presented in the production account, the income approach in the generation of income account, and the expenditure approach

---

[6]In a number of countries, an alternative measure known as gross national product (GNP) is emphasized. It is equal to GDP plus net primary income flows with the rest of the world. In the *1993 SNA*, GNP is more correctly referred to as gross national income (GNI).

Production -

in a rearrangement of the goods and services account. Before describing the approaches, the _1993 SNA_ defines GDP as indicated below.

Defining GDP

GDP is the sum of _value added_ produced by all institutional units resident in the domestic economy plus the value of _taxes less subsidies on products_. In the definition, _value added_ equals the value of output less the values of goods and services (intermediate consumption) used to produce this output. Also in the definition, _taxes on products_[7] have a direct bearing on measuring GDP.

In its treatment of taxes, the _1993 SNA_ distinguishes between taxes levied because production takes place but that _cannot be related to a specific product_, and taxes levied on the value or volume of _specific_ products. Examples of the nonspecific product taxes are import duties (_taxes on products_) and payroll taxes (_other taxes on production_), whereas a sales tax is an example of a specific product tax.

Although users sometimes think of GDP as equal to the sum of the value added by resident producers, they should be mindful that value added excludes taxes on products, whereas the value of goods and services includes them. Thus, to ensure that the value of supply equals the value of use, analysts need to add back the taxes on products to the value added.

In addition, _other taxes on production_ have a bearing on measurement when value added is summed at _basic prices_—the preferred valuation of output of a producing unit in the national accounts. The basic price includes other taxes on production payable by the producer, because units treat them as production costs needing to be covered by the price. The basic price excludes taxes on products, because the unit considers the taxes income for the government, not the producer.

To understand the basic principles for measuring GDP, let us assume that a country produces wheat, cotton, steel, flour, bread, cloth, dresses, cigarettes, and automobiles. How is this production to be accounted? An establishment or enterprise may use some of the goods produced by other establishments as its inputs. Wheat is used in the production of flour, cotton in the production of cloth, and so on. To avoid any duplication in accounting, recorders must subtract from the value of the output of all resi-

---

[7]The discussion has been couched in terms of taxes on production but applies equally to subsidies on production. Subsidies are effectively a negative tax.

dent producing units their intermediate consumption (the inputs of goods and services used up in the process). The measure would be of the *value added* to intermediate consumption to generate the output.

Production Approach

The above approach to measuring GDP is termed the *production approach* and is presented in the production account of the system. GDP is termed gross because no deduction has been made for the consumption of fixed capital (depreciation) used in production. It is useful to note that GDP is measured at market prices.[8]

Income Approach

An alternative approach to measuring GDP is to sum the incomes generated by the productive process. Called the *income approach,* the method involves summing compensation of employees, taxes less subsidies on production, and the operating surplus/mixed income of the producer. *Mixed income* simply refers to the surplus owned by households as producers—economists consider it a combination of compensation of employees and operating surplus. *Compensation of employees*, a broad term, includes not only wages and salaries paid directly but also various indirect benefits of employment, such as employers' contributions to social security and pension funds. This approach is presented in the generation of income account of the system.

Expenditure Approach

A third method of calculating GDP is to sum the final use of the output produced. Called the *expenditure approach,* this involves a summation and a subtraction: (1) summing the values of (a) final consumption (that is, goods and services used up by individual households or the community to satisfy their individual or collective needs or wants), (b) gross capital formation (that is, gross fixed capital formation, changes in inventories, and net acquisition of valuables), and (c) exports of goods and services and (2) subtracting imports of goods and services. *Gross fixed capital formation* is measured by the total value of a producer's acquisitions, less disposals, of fixed assets during the accounting period plus certain addi-

---

[8]GDP at factor cost is not a concept used explicitly in the system.

TABLE 2. GOODS AND SERVICES ACCOUNT

Resources		Uses	
Output, basic prices	3,604	Intermediate consumption	1,883
Taxes less subsidies on		Final consumption expenditure	
products	133	Government	368
Imports of goods and services	499	Households and NPISH	1,031
		Gross capital formation	
		Gross fixed capital formation	376
		Changes in inventories	28
		Acquisitions less disposals of	
		valuables	10
		Exports of goods and services	540
Total supply	**4,236**	**Total use**	**4,236**

tions to the value of nonproduced assets realized by the productive activity of institutional units.

The expenditure approach is based on the fact that the total supply of goods and services must be allocated to a use: for intermediate/final consumption of goods and services, fixed capital formation, inventories, valuables, and exports.[9] It involves a rearrangement of the goods and services account of the *1993 SNA*, as in Table 2.[10]

From this account (see Table 2), a well-known identity is readily apparent between the resources and uses of the total supply of goods and services. That is, the total resources consist of the sum of output and imports, and total uses consist of the sum of consumption, investment, and exports.

Moving intermediate consumption from the right-hand side of the account to the left as a negative resource, while moving imports from the left-hand side to the right as a negative use, results in both sides now summing to GDP (Table 3). In Table 3, the left-hand side presents the production approach and the right-hand side presents the expenditure approach.

In algebraic terms, this relationship can be presented as $GDP = C + I + G + (X - M)$, where C is final consumption expenditure of households and

---

[9]The third category of capital formation, net acquisition (that is, acquisitions less disposals) of valuables, was introduced in the *1993 SNA*. Valuables (such as precious stones and metals and paintings) are used as "stores of value" and not for consumption or production.

[10]Tables 2 through 6 in this chapter include sample data entries based on the data examples given in the *1993 SNA*.

TABLE 3. GROSS DOMESTIC PRODUCT

Production Approach		Expenditure Approach	
Output, basic prices	3,604	Final consumption expenditure	
Less intermediate consumption	−1,883	Government (*G*)	368
Gross value added	**1,721**	Households and NPISH (*C*)	1,031
		Gross capital formation (*I*)	
		Gross fixed capital formation	376
Taxes less subsidies on products	133	Change in inventories	28
		Acquisitions less disposals of	
		valuables	10
		Exports of goods and services (*X*)	540
		Less imports of goods and	
		services (*M*)	−499
GDP	**1,854**	**GDP**	**1,854**

NPISH, *I* is gross capital formation, *G* is final consumption expenditure of government, *X* is exports of goods and services, and *M* is imports of goods and services.

Although analysts greatly emphasize measuring GDP, the details of the *1993 SNA*'s sequence of accounts present a good deal more useful information as well. In essence, users can compile the accounts for each institutional sector in the economy (for example, general government) and for the economy as a whole.[11] Such sectoral accounts usefully inform users about the structure of an economy and changes in that structure over time.

Details: The Sequence of Accounts

As noted earlier, the main sequence of accounts is the current, accumulation, and balance sheet accounts. Current accounts consist of production and income accounts; accumulation accounts consist of capital, financial, and other economic flow accounts; and balance sheets present the stock information.

Further, each account includes a balancing item—a residual from the transactions recorded on the two sides of the account. The balancing item from one account is carried forward as the first item in the following account, thereby making the sequence of accounts an articulated whole. The

---

[11]The sequence of accounts can also be applied at the level of the individual institutional unit, which makes it a very powerful compilation and verification framework.

main balancing item from the current accounts is *saving*, and the main balancing item from the capital account is *NL/B*, which is also the balancing item for the financial account.

We begin with the current accounts (Table 4).

Current Accounts

Production accounts

The *production account* emphasizes *value added* measured on both a gross and a net basis. Gross value added is derived as the difference between the value of output and the value of goods and services (intermediate consumption) used to produce this output. Intermediate consumption does not cover the progressive wear and tear of fixed capital, which is recorded as a separate transaction (consumption of fixed capital), making the difference between the alternative gross and net balancing items.[12] Users can derive these balancing items for each institutional sector. For the economy as a whole, after allowing for taxes less subsidies on products, the balancing item is GDP—the sum of gross value added for each sector—and the net balancing item is *net domestic product*.[13]

Income accounts

The *income accounts* are the generation of income, allocation of primary income, secondary distribution of income, and use of income.

The *generation of income account* shows the *primary incomes* that originate from production (primary income accrues to units from their involvement in production or their ownership of assets). That is, the account shows how value added is allocated from the producers' point of view. The account shows the charges producers have to meet—out of value added (as a resource)—to the government through taxes less subsidies on production and to employed labor as compensation of employees. The balancing item is *operating surplus/mixed income*.

The *allocation of primary income account* focuses on the *recipients* of primary incomes from production, as well as on the recording of the distribution of income from the ownership of financial assets, land, and

---

[12]Accounting for the consumption of fixed capital in any account in this sequence will result in a net measure for the balancing item.

[13]Users may be also interested in information on an industry breakdown of GDP and its components. SUTs provide this information, discussed in the annex to this chapter.

TABLE 4. CURRENT ACCOUNTS

Uses		Resources	
Production account			
Intermediate consumption	1,883	Output, basic prices	3,604
Domestic product, gross (GDP)	*1,854*	Taxes less subsidies on products	133
Less consumption of fixed capital	−222		
Domestic product, net	*1,632*		
Generation of income account			
Compensation of employees	762	GDP	**1,854**
Taxes less subsidies on production			
Taxes less subsidies on products	133		
Other taxes less subsidies on production	58		
Gross operating surplus/mixed income	*901*		
Allocation of primary income account			
Property income payable	391	Gross operating surplus/mixed income	**901**
National income, gross	*1,883*	Compensation of employees	766
		Taxes less subsidies on production	191
		Property income receivable	416
Secondary distribution of income account			
Current taxes on income, wealth, etc. payable	212	National income, gross	**1,883**
Social contributions payable	322	Current taxes on income, wealth, etc. receivable	213
Social benefits payable	332	Social contributions receivable	322
Other current transfers payable	269	Social benefits receivable	332
National disposable income, gross	*1,854*	Other current transfers receivable	239
Use of income account			
Final consumption	1,399	National disposable income, gross	**1,854**
Saving, gross	*455*		
Less consumption of fixed capital	−222		
Saving, net	*233*		

Note: The system described is for transactions between resident units in which both ends of the transaction are recorded—their resource and use. But since one end of some transactions may be a use or resource of nonresident units, then to close the system, the national accounts has a "rest of the world" segment, not illustrated here. For example, compensation of employees in the generation of income account may be paid to resident and nonresident employees, but compensation of employees in the allocation of income account is that received by resident households only, but would include income received from nonresident units.

subsoil assets (property income). Because domestic flows of property income are resources for some sectors and uses for others, they appear on both sides of the account.[14] For the total economy, *national income* is the balancing item.[15]

The *secondary distribution of income account* shows how the balance of primary incomes of sectors (national income) is transformed into its *national disposable income* by the receipt and payment of current transfers. By definition, current transfers cover current taxes on income, wealth, and so forth; social contributions and benefits; and other current transfers. Because these transfers are resources for some sectors and uses for others, they appear on both sides of the account. For a measure of final consumption and saving, analysts can use the balancing item *national disposable income*. It equals national income plus net current transfers from the rest of the world.

The *use of income account* shows how national disposable income is allocated between final consumption and *saving*, which is the balancing item.

The next section reviews the accumulation accounts—the capital and financial accounts (Table 5) and the other economic flows (Table 6).

Accumulation Accounts

Capital account

The *capital account* records the transactions—acquisitions/disposals— of nonfinancial assets and capital transfers (see Table 5). The right-hand side of the account comprises saving and net capital transfers (that is, changes in net worth owing to saving and capital transfers). The left-hand side shows transactions in nonfinancial assets.

If, in the capital account, the aggregate of saving and capital transfers exceeds the net acquisition of nonfinancial assets, the balancing item is *net lending* (+), which measures the surplus an economy has lent to the rest of the world. On the other hand, if saving and capital transfers, and so forth, are

---

[14]Compensation of employees is recorded in both the generation and allocation of income accounts. In the former, it would be compensation paid to resident and nonresident households, whereas for the latter it would be compensation received by the resident household sector.

[15]*National income* is commonly defined as GDP plus net primary income receivable from the rest of the world.

TABLE 5. CAPITAL AND FINANCIAL ACCOUNTS

Changes in Assets		Changes in Liabilities and Net Worth	
Capital account			
Gross fixed capital formation	376	Saving, net	**233**
Less consumption of fixed capital	–222	Capital transfers, receivable	62
Change in inventories	28	Capital transfers, payable	–65
Net lending (+)/borrowing (–)	*38*	**Changes in net worth due to saving and capital transfers[1]**	**230**
Financial account			
Net acquisition of financial assets	641	Net incurrence of liabilities	603
Monetary gold and SDRs	–1	Currency and deposits	132
Currency and deposits	119	Securities other than shares	123
Securities other than shares	138	Loans	217
Loans	244	Shares and other equity	43
Shares and other equity	44	Insurance technical reserves	36
Insurance technical reserves	36	Financial derivatives	0
Financial derivatives	0	Other accounts payable	52
Other accounts receivable	61		
		Net lending (+)/net borrowing (–)	**38**

[1]This item is not a balancing item but corresponds to the total of the right-hand side of the capital account.

insufficient to finance the net acquisition of nonfinancial assets, the balancing item is *net borrowing (–),* which corresponds to the deficit the economy has been obliged to finance by borrowing from the rest of the world.

Financial account

The *financial account* shows how an economy undertakes the NL/B through transactions in financial assets and liabilities (see Table 5). The account is classified by financial instrument, with the net acquisition of financial assets shown on the left-hand side, and the net incurrence of liabilities on the right. Users are often interested in more detail on the financial flows taking place in an economy than is provided at the aggregate level of the financial account for the whole economy, and this is illustrated in the detailed list of instruments making up the assets and liabilities.

Other economic flows

Other economic flows appear in the *other changes in volume of assets account* and the *revaluation account* (see Table 6). The other changes in volume

TABLE 6. BALANCE SHEET AND ACCUMULATION ACCOUNTS

Assets		Liabilities and Net Worth	
Opening balance sheet			
Nonfinancial assets	9,922	Liabilities	6,298
Financial assets	6,792	**Net worth**	**10,416**
Changes in balance sheet (accumulation accounts)			
1. Transactions			
Acquisitions less disposals of		Net incurrence of liabilities	603
nonfinancial assets	192		
Net acquisition of financial assets	641	**Changes in net worth due to saving**	
		and capital transfers	**230**
2. Other changes in volume of assets account			
Changes in assets		Changes in liabilities	–2
Nonfinancial	10	**Changes in net worth due to other**	
Financial	5	**changes in volume of assets**	**17**
3. Revaluation account			
Nominal holding gains (+)/losses (–)		Nominal holding gains (+)/losses (–)	
Nonfinancial assets	280	liabilities	76
Financial assets	84	**Changes in net worth due to**	
		nominal holding gains/losses	**288**
Closing balance sheet			
Nonfinancial assets	10,404	Liabilities	6,976
Financial assets	7,522	**Net worth**	**10,951**

of assets account includes events such as the discovery of new oil reserves, destruction of assets by national catastrophes, and uncompensated seizures of assets. And the revaluation account includes holding gains and losses owing to price changes in the assets or liabilities over the accounting period.

Balance Sheets

The *balance sheets* show the values of the stock of assets and liabilities for the economy at the beginning and end of the period. They inform users, therefore, about the types of assets owned by an economy and the structure of its debt and other liabilities. The difference between the total stock of assets and the stock of liabilities is the *net worth* of the economy.

The change in the balance sheet between the opening and closing positions is explained fully by the transactions (of the capital and financial accounts) and the other economic flows (the other changes in volume of assets account and revaluation account) (see Table 6).

29

Other Related Issues in the *1993 SNA*

Other related issues include the volume and real income measures, quarterly national accounts (QNA) data, important boundaries (production boundary, asset boundary, and current and capital transfers), labor force indicators, multifactor productivity, environmental and economic accounting, and informal sector and illegal activities. Finally, an annex illustrates supply and use tables.

Volume and Real Income Measures

One of the questions users expect national accountants to answer is, "By how much has GDP changed?" Another is, "What has happened to the 'real' income of the country?" Volume and price indices provide some answers to such questions. They provide information over and above the growth rates calculated from GDP measured at current (nominal) prices. As users are aware, those particular growth rates are of little analytical use because they include both price and volume changes, and only the latter are generally of interest to the user.

GDP volume and constant price measures

With volume and constant price measures, users can factor changes over time in the value of goods and services into two components—changes in their prices and changes in their volumes. Measuring the volume, while holding prices constant at some base period, provides the constant price value of the aggregate. Users may achieve this either by deflating the current period value with an appropriate price index (deflation) or by extrapolating the base period value with an appropriate indicator of volume or quantity change. Users often choose components of the producer price index (PPI), consumer price index (CPI), and export and import price indices (XMPIs) as the deflators. These indices are also valuable as measures of price changes in their own right (see Boxes 4–6).

To obtain a volume series of GDP at the constant prices of some base year, users can combine estimates of expenditure at constant prices (consumption, capital formation, and exports) less imports at constant prices. This involves deflating each component (and subcomponent) by relevant price indices. Or it involves using alternative extrapolation methods, depending on available source data for each component (for example, volume changes of related output or inputs as indicators).

30

Box 4. Producer Price Index

A producer price index (PPI) measures the rate of change in the prices of goods and services bought and sold by producers. It usually includes mining, manufacturing, public utilities, agriculture, forestry, and fishing but can extend to construction and services. It is a key statistic for economic and business decision making and inflation monitoring. An *output* PPI measures the rate of change in the prices of products sold as they leave the producer. An *input* PPI measures the rate of change in the prices of the inputs of goods and services purchased by the producer.

The main uses of the PPI are as (1) a short-term indicator of inflationary trends; (2) indexation in legal contracts in both the public and private sectors, particularly for more detailed PPI components; (3) compilation of other inflation measures such as an export price index or the final expenditure price index; (4) an analytical tool for businesses and researchers; and (5) national accounts deflation.

Collecting data for PPIs is not trivial. In practical terms, PPIs require sampling—from a representative sample of establishments—a set of well-defined products whose overall price changes represent those of the millions of transactions taking place. Statistical offices then monitor the prices of these same products periodically (usually monthly) and weight their price changes according to their relative revenue.

The *Producer Price Index Manual: Theory and Practice* (ILO and others, 2004a) provides clear, up-to-date guidance on the concepts, uses, methods, and economic theory of the PPI, including information on classifications, sources, compilation techniques, and analytical uses of the PPI. The *Manual*'s conceptual framework derives from the *1993 SNA* and recent developments in index number theory.

To obtain a volume series of GDP at constant prices from the production approach, users must sum, for each period, the gross value added, measured at the (constant) prices of the base year, of producers in the economy and then add a "real" measure of taxes less subsidies on products. To measure gross value added of a unit, industry, or sector, at constant prices, users can subtract intermediate consumption at constant prices from output at constant prices. Known as the double-deflation approach, this method takes into account differences over time in the ratio of intermediate consumption to output as well as price changes of output and intermediate consumption.

However, sufficient data are not always available, and a second-best alternative would be to extrapolate base-year value added by an output

Box 5. Consumer Price Index

The consumer price index (CPI) measures, usually as a monthly series, the overall rate of change in the prices of goods and services consumed by households. Analysts also widely use it as a proxy for a general index of inflation for the economy as a whole, partly because of the frequency and timeliness with which it is produced. It has become a key statistic for the purpose of economic policymaking, especially monetary policy. It is often specified in legislation and in a wide variety of contracts as the appropriate measure of inflation for the purpose of adjusting payments (such as wages, rents, interest, and social security benefits) for the effects of inflation. It can therefore have substantial and wide-ranging financial implications for governments and businesses, as well as for households. Another use is for national accounts deflation.

The prices used to compile the CPI are of selected representative items of different product groups, monitored each month from a representative sample of shops or other retail outlets. The usual method of calculation is to measure the average period-to-period price changes for each selected item and then weight these item price changes by the relative amounts that households spend on them. It is not unusual for agencies to monitor more than 100,000 price quotes each month. CPIs are official statistics usually produced by national statistical offices, ministries of labor, or central banks. They are published as quickly as possible, typically about 10–15 days after the end of the most recent month or quarter.

The *Consumer Price Index Manual: Theory and Practice* (ILO and others, 2004b) provides guidelines for statistical offices and other agencies responsible for constructing CPIs and explains in depth the methods used to calculate a CPI. It also examines the underlying economic and statistical concepts and principles needed for making methodological choices efficiently and cost-effectively and for appreciating the full implications of those choices.

volume index. A third-best alternative would be to deflate current-period value added by a price index for output (single deflation).

In measuring a GDP series at constant base-period prices, users need to ensure that the price index used for deflation—or the volume index used for base-period extrapolation—uses relative expenditure/revenue values in the base period as weights in their aggregation. However, such weights will become out of date, and users should regularly update them to reflect changes in production/consumption patterns.

It follows that users need to update the base period(s) frequently and link the resulting series. The *1993 SNA* expresses a preference for annual chain-

Box 6. Export and Import Price Indices

Export and import price indices (XMPIs) for a country measure the rate of change over time in the prices of traded goods and services. A country's *export* price index measures the rate of change in the prices of goods and services sold to foreign buyers by residents of that country. A country's *import* price index measures the rate of change in the prices of goods and services purchased from abroad by residents of that country.

These foreign trade indices, as measures of both price and volume changes, have many uses. The most important of these are their use in government economic policy, analysis of competitiveness, conclusion of trade contracts, measurement and forecasting of inflation, analysis of exchange rate, and compilation of national accounts.

Surrogates for price indices are sometimes unit-value indices—a readily available by-product of the collection of trade data by customs authorities. However, in this respect, unit-value indices are recognized as prone to bias. Survey-based XMPIs are the preferred alternative. Yet in practical terms, these require sampling, from a representative set of establishments, a set of well-defined commodities whose overall price changes represent those of the millions of transactions taking place. Statistical offices then monitor the prices of these same commodities periodically (usually monthly) and weight their price changes according to their relative trade shares. As with the CPI and PPI indices, this is a complex exercise.

The *Export and Import Price Index Manual: Theory and Practice* (IMF, forthcoming) will provide clear, up-to-date guidance on the concepts, uses, methods, and economic theory of the XMPIs, including information on classification, sources, compilation techniques, and analytical uses. The *Manual*'s conceptual framework derives from the *1993 SNA* and recent developments in index number theory.

ing, with a note that base-year updates should be made at least about every five years. In preparing annual chained indices (extrapolating a GDP series by volume indices or deflating it by price indices that have benefited from updated weights), users should no longer describe the series as at the constant prices of the base period. The resulting series is a volume measure of GDP.

Chained indices for subcomponents, such as industries, do not aggregate consistently to higher levels—say, to GDP. Yet these chained indices are conceptually more sound than fixed-base indices, which may add up but yield a worse estimate. Chained indices are, however, biased when used for high-frequency—say, monthly—volatile data.

Dividing the series of GDP at nominal (current) prices by the series of GDP at constant prices will result in the GDP (implicit price) deflator—a measure of the cost of goods purchased by households, government, industry, and so forth.[16] The CPI (see Box 5) covers household expenditure, while the coverage of GDP has been explained to extend beyond this. Further, the weighting implicit in the GDP deflator may, depending on the method used for the volume index, be quite different from the CPI's base-period weighting.

Real income

Before considering the measures of real income for an economy, users need to understand the difference between GDP at constant prices and real gross domestic income (GDI).[17] GDP at constant prices is a volume measure for *output*. However, the real *income* that residents derive from domestic production depends also on changes in the country's terms of trade. If the prices of a country's exports rise faster than the prices of its imports (that is, the terms of trade improve), then fewer exports are needed to pay for a given volume of imports. Thus, improving the terms of trade in a country makes it possible for that country's residents to purchase an increased volume of goods and services out of the incomes generated by a given level of domestic production.

It follows that when the terms of trade change, the movements in GDP at constant prices and in real GDI may significantly diverge. Economists generally describe this difference as the "trading gain (or loss)." Calculating the trading gain (or loss) is described in Box 7.

In addition to measuring real GDI, countries find it useful to derive the other national accounts aggregates in real terms. For example, in a number of countries, the receipts of workers' remittances from abroad are crucial for domestic demand, and an emphasis on measuring only GDP at constant prices may be misleading. In particular, the real disposable income of such countries may show a very different pattern of growth from their GDP growth because the flow of remittances is affected by developments in the rest of the world.

---

[16]An implicit price deflator for an aggregate, such as GDP, is obtained by dividing the value at current prices by the value at constant prices and multiplying the result by 100.

[17]The term *real GDP* should be avoided. The concern is either with the volume measure of GDP or with real income.

**Box 7. Calculating Trading Gains (Losses) Resulting
from Changes in the Terms of Trade**

The trading gains (losses) are calculated as

$$T = \frac{X - M}{P} - \left(\frac{X}{P_X} - \frac{M}{P_M} \right),$$

where the first term is a measure of the goods and services balance
(exports of goods and services (X) less imports of goods and services (M))
using a single deflator, P, and the second term is the goods and services
balance by taking the difference between a volume (say constant price)
measure of exports and a volume measure of imports—that is, after X and
M have been deflated by respective price indices for exports and imports,
P_X and P_M. Note in the second term how, for example, as export prices
increase slower than import prices, the larger is the sum deducted from the
first term, and the smaller the terms of trade effect. In many economies,
deflated imports may exceed deflated exports, and the second term is
negative. In such cases, it is highly desirable that the economy calculate
the trading loss, because the possibility exists that the loss may offset any
positive growth in GDP.

Note also that the magnitude of the terms of trade effect is contingent on
the deflator in the first term. Experts do not agree on the best deflator to
use for this component. They have suggested both the import price index
and the export price index, depending on whether the balance is negative
or positive. The interpretation of the trading gain would be in terms of
the gain in purchasing power with regard to a respective bundle of such
goods and services. Some argue for a simple average of the import and
export price indices. There is a good case, consistent with the definition
of real national income, for using the implicit deflator for gross domestic
expenditure.

The links between the real income aggregates are as follows:
1. Volume or constant price GDP—the GDP in the current year at prices
   of the base year
   plus the trading gain or loss resulting from changes in the terms of
   trade
2. *Equals* real gross domestic income
   plus real primary incomes from abroad
   minus real primary incomes payable abroad

3. *Equals* real gross national income
   plus real current transfers receivable from abroad
   minus real current transfers payable abroad
4. *Equals* real gross national disposable income.

The deflator used to measure these real income components is not clear, because no deflator can be directly applied to primary incomes and transfers to and from abroad. However, it is important that the deflator be broadly based, and countries often use the implicit price deflator for gross domestic expenditure.[18]

Quarterly National Accounts Data

Another important related feature of macroeconomic statistics is QNA data. National accounts data must be timely to be useful for macroeconomic planning. QNA are a natural progression once countries have established annual accounts. For QNA, the potential scope is the whole of the *1993 SNA* sequence of accounts. Although GDP and its components are the usual important starting point, the prerequisites of such accounts are the timely and accurate quarterly source data directly covering a high proportion of the totals.

National data compilers should make QNA consistent with the annual equivalents, partly for the convenience of users and partly—and more fundamentally—for the benchmarking process. The benchmarking process incorporates the information from annual data into the quarterly estimates. Also, data compilers need to use revisions to allow them to release data on a timely basis and to subsequently incorporate new data.

Important Boundaries

Note that economies use some important boundaries to define the scope and treatment of events that occur within the economy. These boundaries are the *production boundary*, defining the scope of productive activity; the *asset boundary*, distinguishing transactions in assets from income and expenditure; and the *boundary* between *current* and *capital* transfers, impacting the measure of saving.

Production boundary

The definition of production used in the national accounts determines the scope of the activities covered and the size of the economy measured in

---

[18]Gross domestic expenditure is GDP measured by the expenditure approach.

the accounts. The system defines production in general terms as an activity in which a unit uses inputs to produce goods and services of a kind that can be provided to other units, either individually or collectively, with or without change.

The location of the production boundary is a compromise, but a deliberate one that takes account of the needs of most users. The location strikes a balance between users' desire to make the accounts as comprehensive as possible and the need to prevent flows used for analyzing market behavior and disequilibria from being swamped by nonmonetary values. Thus, the boundary of production in the *1993 SNA* encompasses

- The production of all goods by a unit, including for own use;
- The production of services by a unit that are supplied to other units;
- The own-account production of housing services by owner-occupiers; and
- The production of domestic and personal services through the employment of paid domestic staff.

As a general principle, the boundary includes production of *goods* for own use but excludes own-produced *services.* That is, it includes goods produced for own use because units can switch goods between market and nonmarket use. However, it excludes own-produced services, because units consume them as they produce them. For example, if the boundary restricted production to only those goods and services produced by one unit and sold to another, then it would impractically exclude subsistence production (produced and consumed by the same unit). On the other hand, if production were to cover all goods and services, then it would cover subsistence production but would needlessly cover services provided by a unit to itself, such as the preparation of meals, cleaning, household repairs, child care, and so forth.

All these activities are productive in an economic sense. However, including them in the system is not simply a matter of estimating economic values for their output. If analysts are to assign values to the output, then they also need to estimate concomitant measures of income and consumption. Clearly, the economic significance of these nonmonetary flows differs from that of monetary flows. For example, incomes generated by them are automatically tied to the consumption of the output produced, having little relevance for analysts in assessing market disequilibria in the economy.

Regarding sectors and the boundary, the financial and nonfinancial corporate sectors produce most goods and services. However, it is not unusual for the household sector to also produce a great number, particularly, but not exclusively, in developing countries.

Financial corporations may charge explicitly for their services. Under such circumstances, analysts find it straightforward to measure their output. However, financial intermediaries and insurance corporations may also charge indirectly for their services, and analysts must estimate their output. For example, financial intermediaries levy a service charge as part of the interest they pay on their borrowing (including deposits) and the interest they earn on their lending. This is known as the financial intermediation services indirectly measured (FISIM) charge, and analysts need to allocate it to the users of the financial services.

In addition, analysts need to adjust actual interest flows to take account of the service charge. For example, the premiums that insurance corporations receive include a service charge, which analysts can broadly estimate by subtracting from premiums the value of claims and changes in any reserves that belong to the policyholders.

Households essentially engage in earning income from labor services, using it for consumption and saving. However, households often engage in production that cannot be assigned to a separate institutional unit. In particular, in agriculture, part of the output is often consumed by the farmer without passing through the market. Analysts must estimate such output and consumption and include it in GDP. In developing countries, part of the population may live in the subsistence sector, and such own-account production may be quite large.

As for the general government and NPISH—for example, trade unions and charities—they engage in producing goods and services that satisfy either individual or collective needs. Although these sectors may provide such services free, the production boundary still includes them.

Asset boundary

The *asset boundary* includes financial and fixed assets and nonproduced (naturally occurring) assets over which effective ownership rights are exercised, privately or otherwise. The coverage of assets is limited to those entities subject to ownership rights and from which their owners may derive economic benefits by holding them or using them in economic activity. The owners may derive such benefits by using the assets such as buildings and machinery in production. Other assets may provide benefits in the form of property incomes (such as dividends and interest), and still others may be held as a store of value (for example, precious metals).

The boundary includes, as the acquisition of an asset, the expenditure on mineral exploration, on the grounds that the information gained from the exploration is likely to allow the enterprise to derive future economic benefits.

Major renovations, reconstructions, and enlargements of existing assets are considered to be capital formation because they increase the performance or productive capacity of the asset involved. Regular repair and maintenance, however, are treated as current costs of production.

The asset boundary is important for helping users determine whether to record a transaction as income/expenditure in the current accounts of the system or as assets/liabilities in the accumulation accounts. As such, the boundary directly affects how users measure balances of the current accounts—GDP, national income, and savings.

Boundary between current and capital transfers

The national accounts include transfers—that is, transactions between institutional units, with one unit (say, the government) receiving nothing directly in return from the other. All transfers increase the net worth of the recipient unit.

The *1993 SNA* draws an important distinction between current and capital transfers. Current transfers contribute to disposable income (and saving), whereas capital transfers link the transfer to an asset. The payment of an inheritance tax would be an example of a capital transfer; the receipt of a social security benefit would be a current transfer. Debt forgiveness received by a country would make that country better off. However, it would be misleading to show that its saving has increased. The *1993 SNA* records debt forgiveness in the capital account as a capital transfer.

Labor Force Indicators

Another important feature of macroeconomic statistics is better knowledge of developments in the labor market. That is, with aggregate data on employment (persons employed, hours worked, earnings, and so forth), analysts have crucial inputs for assessing economic performance. Oftentimes, with these indicators, they may gauge the effectiveness of labor market policy, using data on labor market demand (employment, job vacancies, labor costs) and labor market supply (unemployment, labor force participation).

Box 8. Labor Statistics

Labor statistics extensively cover employment and unemployment from both economic and social standpoints.

A fundamental concept is the *economically active* population—defined as all persons who, during a reference period, furnish the supply of labor for the production of goods and services, as defined by the *1993 SNA*.

The currently economically active population (also known as the labor force) gives a measure of the number of persons furnishing the supply of labor at a given time. It comprises two mutually exclusive categories—employed and unemployed. For practical reasons, the labor force statistics framework specifies a minimum age for measuring economic activity—thus defining the working-age population (which may differ from country to country).

Employed persons are those above the minimum specified age who performed some work for pay, profit, or family gain during the specified reference period or who had a paid job or an enterprise but were temporarily not at work for some specified reason.

The international standards further specify that, for operational purposes, the notion of "some work" may be interpreted as work for at least one hour. This criterion is intended to cover all types of work, especially types having irregular features, and is a necessary criterion if total employment is to correspond to aggregate production.

The international standard definition of unemployment is based on three criteria to be satisfied simultaneously. *Unemployed* persons are those who are

• Without work (were not in paid employment or self-employment as specified by the definition of employment),

To draw up labor statistics, statisticians use business surveys, household surveys, and administrative sources. Successive conferences of labor statisticians under the auspices of the International Labor Organization (ILO) have developed concepts and definitions of labor statistics (Box 8).

Multifactor Productivity

In macroeconomics, two useful measurement tools are *productivity comparisons* and *productivity indices*. Productivity *comparisons* (comparing productivity for a given period between, say, economic sectors, institutions, or regions) use the ratio of output over inputs. To measure output and inputs, analysts may use nominal and/or quantity terms, such as value

- Currently available for work (were available for paid employment or self-employment during the reference period), and
- Seeking work (had taken specific steps in a specified recent period to seek paid employment or self-employment).

Persons in the working-age population who satisfy neither the definition of employment nor that of unemployment are classified as *economically inactive* or not in the labor force.

Three principal *classifications* are used to categorize data collected in surveys of the economically active population:

- *Status in employment.* Persons may be classified as an employee (receives payment for work in wages, salaries, commission, tips, piece rates, or pay in-kind), employer (with one or more employees), own-account worker, unpaid family worker, and other categories of nonemployees.
- *Branch of economic activity (industry).* Industry refers to the activity (kind of goods produced or services supplied) of the economic unit in which the employed person worked.
- *Occupation.* Occupation refers to the kind of work done during the reference period, irrespective of the industry or the person's status in employment.

The ILO's Bureau of Statistics has extensive material on definitions, concepts, and classification standards available on its website (http://www.ilo.org/public/english/bureau/stat/index.htm) and in printed publications.

added divided by hours worked. Productivity *indices* track trends in the ratio of output over input. Analysts have produced variants of productivity indices by considering gross or net output measures and input measures of differing kind and scope (see Box 9 for more details).

In terms of these tools, *output* may be output volume (the volume of gross production), or it may be value added volume (the volume of net production after accounting for intermediate consumption). The latter measure has particular appeal to policymakers—it is related directly to GDP, which, as discussed earlier, is the sum of the value added produced by the establishments resident in an economic territory. This, in particular, makes productivity measures relevant to a range of economic policy considerations. For example, rapid growth in GDP volume accompanied by a

Box 9. Productivity Indices

The most widely used productivity measures focus on labor productivity, or output over labor input, where output is either gross or net:

$$\text{Gross labor productivity} = \frac{\text{Output volume index}}{\text{Labor input volume index}}$$

$$\text{Net labor productivity} = \frac{\text{Value added volume}}{\text{Labor input volume index}}$$

Productivity measures may gauge labor input as a stock or adjust it for its flow of services in terms of hours worked, education, occupation, gender, and other such compositions. However, analysts find the productivity measures that take into account the full array of inputs more useful than the single input measures, such as labor productivity.

The input scope of these multifactor productivity (MFP) indices may be defined in two ways according to the output concept:

$$\text{Gross MFP} = \frac{\text{Output volume index}}{\text{Primary (including labor) and intermediate input volume index}}$$

$$\text{Net MFP} = \frac{\text{Value added volume index}}{\text{Primary (including labor) input volume index}}$$

The measures just described presume that the economy operates at constant, unitary *returns to scale*—that is, scaling inputs by a given factor results in an increase in potential output by the same factor. Economists have noted that returns to scale affect productivity measures, both single factor and multifactor. That is, decreasing the returns to scale blunts the impact of growth in inputs in the denominator of the productivity index, and thus input growth offsets output growth to a lesser extent than under constant, unitary returns to scale. Increasing the returns to scale magnifies the impact of the growth of the inputs in the denominator and thus offsets the growth of output in the numerator more than under constant, unitary returns to scale. The returns-to-scale concept is the main unknown parameter in computing productivity indices, though economists may determine it simply from measured prices and quantities of inputs and outputs under decreasing or constant returns to scale. Most published indicators make no returns-to-scale adjustment, thus assuming constant, unitary returns to scale.

When implementing MFP indices, economies use index numbers to aggregate the relative changes in many types of outputs, intermediate inputs, and primary inputs typical of most economies and captured at some level of detail by the compiling statistical systems. Multifactor productivity indices generally use the so-called Törnqvist formula, because it has exceptional index number properties from a microeconomic point of view and thus is in the class of formulas Diewert (1976) terms *superlative*.

productivity increase will cause less demand pressure on inputs (and thus less cost-push inflation) than rapid growth in the absence of a productivity increase.

The OECD manual *Measuring Productivity* (2001) gives users additional guidance on measuring productivity growth at the aggregate and industry level.

Environmental and Economic Accounting

Increased recognition of the need to sustain economic development has generated a growing demand for data that highlight how the economy and the environment interact. Depletion of subsoil assets, depletion of fisheries, and damage to the physical environment give rise to serious policy concerns, increasing needs for data and analytical accounting frameworks to help policymakers develop and monitor sound policies.

Such considerations have an impact on welfare extending beyond the boundaries of the *1993 SNA,* and the United Nations' System of Environmental and Economic Accounting (SEEA; UN and others, 2003; see also UN, 2004) provides a common framework for economic and environmental information, permitting analysts to consistently assess the contribution of the environment to the economy and the impact of the economy on the environment. The UN's website provides extensive material on definitions, concepts, and classification standards for environmental and economic accounting.

The Informal Sector and Illegal Activities

One of many issues under consideration in a current review of the *1993 SNA* is more detail on the treatment of the informal economy and illegal activities. The *1993 SNA* does not adequately cover such economic activity; other handbooks cover some of it. For example, the *1993 SNA* makes no methodological recommendations per se on the informal sector, aside from referring (*1993 SNA,* paragraph 4.159) to ILO guidelines on employment in the sector. And it recommends little on illegal activities (*1993 SNA,* paragraphs 6.30–6.33). Yet the informal sector and illegal activities can account for a substantial portion of economic activity, especially in developing and transition countries.

Draft papers, handbooks, and guidelines on the subject are available (for example, see OECD and others, 2002).

Annex: Supply and Use Tables

The illustration of the goods and services account in Table 2 showed for the total economy how total supply (output at basic prices plus taxes less subsidies on products plus imports) equals total use at purchasers' prices (intermediate consumption plus final consumption plus capital formation plus exports). Supply and use tables (SUTs) disaggregate this presentation to present the data at a commodity and industry level.

SUTs are rectangular matrices. They consist of a supply table, with products in the rows and producing industries[19] in the columns, and a use table, with the same products in the rows but intermediate consumption (by industry) and final uses in the columns.

SUTs serve two purposes—statistical and analytical. For statistical use, they facilitate the checking of consistency among statistics on the flow of goods and services obtained from quite different statistical sources, such as industrial surveys, household expenditure inquiries, investment surveys, and foreign trade. As such, they provide an appropriate framework for economists to calculate much of the production data included in the national accounts and identify weaknesses in the underlying data. For the analytic purpose, economists can directly integrate SUTs into macroeconomic models of the economy, converting them into square input-output tables to study the link between final demand and industry output.

Economists traditionally refer to compiling detailed product flows—to verify the estimates of commodity use—as the commodity-flow method. Using an economy's basic statistics on the supply and use of goods and services, it involves four basic steps:

- Estimating supply at basic prices for commodities (or commodity groupings),
- Adjusting these estimates to purchaser prices,
- Estimating the uses of the commodities, and
- Comparing the results.

Economists obtain the full power of this method when they independently estimate different uses of the commodity that they then reconcile

---

[19]Institutional units may engage in several different kinds of productive activity simultaneously. For detailed analysis of production, therefore, the *1993 SNA* recommends that economists partition them into separate establishments, each of which engages in a single type of productive activity at a single location. Industries are then defined as groups of establishments engaged in the same kind of productive activities.

with estimates of its supply. Even when they do not have full information (such as when they have estimated a use residually), the method provides a good check on the "reasonableness" of the data and can help to identify major weaknesses.

The greater the level of detail applied to the matrices, the clearer will be the view presented of the economy. Nonetheless, the usefulness of SUTs in a commodity-flow environment is still apparent even at fairly high levels of aggregation.

III

Balance of Payments and International Investment Position

Like the balance of payments manuals issued by the IMF in 1948, 1950, 1961, and 1977, the fifth edition of the *Balance of Payments Manual* (*BPM5*; IMF, 1993) serves as the international standard for the conceptual framework underlying balance of payments and international investment position (IIP) statistics. This framework assists countries in systematically collecting, organizing, and comparing these statistics across countries.

In drafting the *BPM5*, the authors took great care to harmonize it with the *1993 SNA*. In particular, as was done for the national accounts, they extended the balance of payments framework to encompass transactions, other economic flows, and stocks of external financial assets and liabilities (the IIP).

The international financial crises in the 1990s underscored the importance of reliable and timely statistics, particularly on stock data, as a critical element for assessing a country's external vulnerability. To complement the IIP and to provide specialized but IIP-linked frameworks for analyzing stock positions, the IMF issued the *Coordinated Portfolio Investment Survey Guide* (IMF, 1996b),[20] the *Data Template on International Reserves and Foreign Currency Liquidity, Operational Guidelines, Provisional* (IMF, 1999),[21] and *External Debt Statistics: Guide for Compilers and Users* (BIS and others, 2003).

The following sections review the balance of payments and the IIP. Further, they review several data sets that complement the balance of payments and IIP statistics—external debt statistics and direct investment, portfolio investment, and international reserves.

---

[20]The second edition of the *CPIS Guide* was issued in 2002 (IMF, 2002a).

[21]Provisional reserves template guidelines were issued in 1999. The formal version was issued in 2001 (Kester, 2001).

TABLE 7. BALANCE OF PAYMENTS AND INTERNATIONAL INVESTMENT
POSITION FRAMEWORK

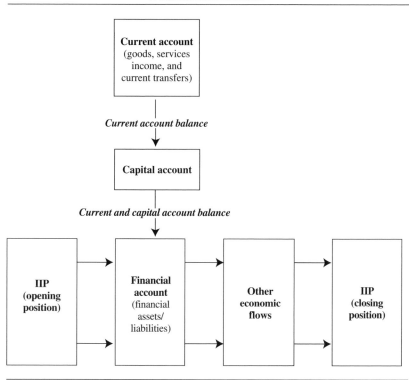

Balance of Payments

Structured similarly to the national accounts, the balance of payments covers all economic events with nonresidents. This section illustrates the three types of balance of payments accounts: the *current account,* recording transactions with nonresidents in goods and services, income, and current transfers; *capital account,* recording transactions in capital transfers and nonproduced nonfinancial assets; and *financial account,* recording transactions in external financial assets and liabilities. The section also throws some light on the terms *surplus* and *deficit,* expressions frequently used in public debate. Further, the section provides examples of the two balance of payments presentations: *standard* and *analytic.*

For the relationship between the balance of payments and the IIP, see Table 7. The IIP statement integrates the opening and closing stocks of

TABLE 8. CURRENT ACCOUNT: STANDARD COMPONENTS

A. Goods and services
   1. Goods
   2. Services
      1. Transportation
      2. Travel
      3. Communications services
      4. Construction services
      5. Insurance services
      6. Financial services
      7. Computer and information services
      8. Royalties and license fees
      9. Other business services
      10. Personal, cultural, and recreational services
      11. Government services, n.i.e.[1]
B. Income
   1. Compensation of employees
   2. Investment income
      2.1 Direct investment
      2.2 Portfolio investment
      2.3 Other investment
C. Current transfers
   1. General government
   2. Other sectors
      2.1 Workers' remittances
      2.2 Other transfers

[1]Not included elsewhere.

external financial assets and liabilities with transactions, revaluations, and other economic flows.

Current Account

The current account's standard components are *goods and services, income*, and *current transfers*. The components, discussed below, are also set out in Table 8. The current account is also closely related to the national accounts.

Goods and services

In the goods and services account, *goods* cover principally exports and imports—as shown in external trade statistics—adjusted for timing, valuation, and coverage in accordance with the change of ownership requirements of the system. Goods include general merchandise, goods for

Box 10. Statistics on International Trade in Services

The statistics on international trade in services (ITS) provide internationally comparable statistics to meet the needs of private and public sectors, including for globalization studies and trade negotiations and agreements. Countries collect ITS information through a coherent conceptual framework within which they can organize the statistics.

ITS statistics take a much broader and detailed view of international trade in services than the conventional balance of payments perspective outlined in *BPM5*. In particular, they (1) classify the services delivered through conventional trade between residents and nonresidents in more detail than is contained in *BPM5*, (2) include a treatment of local delivery of services through a foreign commercial presence, and (3) provide some link between the two systems.

ITS statistics cover four modes through which services may be traded internationally:(1) *cross-border supply*—where suppliers of services in one country supply services to consumers in another country without either party moving into the territory of the other; (2) *consumption abroad*—where a consumer in one country moves to another country to obtain a service; (3) *commercial presence*—where enterprises in an economy supply services through the activities of their foreign affiliates abroad; and (4) *presence of natural persons*—where an individual moves to the country of the consumer to provide a service on his own or employer's behalf.

For guidance on compiling ITS statistics, users may refer to the *Manual on Statistics of International Trade in Services,* issued by an international task force in 2002 (UN and others, 2002).

processing, repairs on goods, goods procured in ports by carriers, and nonmonetary gold. The goods accounts value both exports and imports of goods free on board (f.o.b.) from the country of export, providing for symmetrical valuation.

For *services*, the transportation and insurance service items in the accounts record the costs of shipping the goods between the exporting country and importing country, performed by residents for nonresidents, and vice versa. Other services cover a range of activities, including transportation of passengers, travel, communication, construction, and so forth. For a broader view of trade in services, readers are advised to view statistics on international trade in services (ITS), as summarized in Box 10.

Income

The second component of the current account, *income*, creates a separate category, as in the national accounts, for transactions in primary *incomes*. These transactions comprise compensation of employees (labor income) and investment income—the latter identifying separately direct investment income, portfolio investment, and other investment. The difference between direct investment, portfolio investment, and other investment is discussed below in the context of the financial account.

Current transfers

The third component, *current transfers,* identifies separately, as in the national accounts, the transfers involving the resident general government sector and those involving other resident sectors. In the latter, workers' remittances make up a major component.

The current account balance in particular mirrors the saving and investment behavior of the domestic economy in the national accounts. More information on the linkage between the balance of payments and national accounts aggregates and balances is provided in the chapter on linkages at the end of this pamphlet.

Capital Account

Similar to the capital account of the national accounts, the balance of payments *capital account* records transactions in capital transfers and non-produced, nonfinancial assets. Moreover, when recorders draw a balance to take account of the balance of payments current account and capital account transactions, then that balance equals NL/B with the rest of the world.

The high-level components of the capital account, along with the financial account, are presented in Table 9.

Financial Account

The *financial account* records all transactions in financial assets and liabilities between residents and nonresidents.[22] It records, therefore, the form in which the net lending/borrowing with the rest of the world takes place.

---

[22]The *capital account* concept of previous editions of the balance of payments manual was revised and renamed the *financial account* in *BPM5*.

TABLE 9. CAPITAL AND FINANCIAL ACCOUNTS: STANDARD COMPONENTS

A. Capital account
  1. Capital transfers
    1.1 General government
    1.2 Other sectors
  2. Acquisition/disposal of nonproduced, nonfinancial assets

B. Financial account
  1. Direct investment
    1.1 Abroad
    1.2 In reporting economy
  2. Portfolio investment
    2.1 Assets
      2.1.1 Equity securities
      2.1.2 Debt securities
    2.2 Liabilities
      2.2.1 Equity securities
      2.2.2 Debt securities
  3. Financial derivatives
    3.1 Assets
    3.2 Liabilities
  4. Other investment
    4.1 Assets
      4.1.1 Trade credits
      4.1.2 Loans
      4.1.3 Currency and deposits
      4.1.4 Other assets
    4.2 Liabilities
      4.2.1 Trade credits
      4.2.2 Loans
      4.2.3 Currency and deposits
      4.2.4 Other assets
  5. Reserve assets
    5.1 Monetary gold
    5.2 Special drawing rights (SDRs)
    5.3 Reserve position in the IMF
    5.4 Foreign exchange
    5.5 Other claims

Although the scope of the transactions covered in the financial account is the same as in the national accounts, the classification differs. The financial account transactions are classified using criteria as follows:

1. *By function* (that is, distinguishing the purpose of the investment). The functional categories are direct investment, portfolio investment, financial derivatives, other investment, and reserve assets:

    a. *Direct investment* is characterized by the investor's having an effective voice in the management of an enterprise, identified using a 10 percent equity ownership rule.

    b. *Portfolio investment* refers to investment in debt and equity securities (both usually traded) other than those included in direct investment and reserve assets.

    c. *Financial derivative* instruments are linked to a specific financial instrument, through which specific risks can be traded in their own right in financial markets.[23] They include options, futures contracts, and swaps.

    d. *Other investment* comprises instruments not covered by the other categories, including trade credits, loans, currency and deposits, and other assets/liabilities.

    e. *Reserve assets* consist of external assets readily available to and controlled by the monetary authorities for addressing payments imbalances. The category comprises monetary gold, SDRs, reserve position in the IMF, foreign exchange assets (consisting of currency and deposits, securities, and financial derivatives), and other claims.

2. *By whether the instrument is an asset or liability.*

3. *By the nature of the instrument involved*—equity, debt, trade credit, loans, currency and deposits, and so forth.

4. *By the domestic sector* (in the case of portfolio investment and other investment) *acquiring the assets or incurring the liabilities.* The sectors are monetary authorities, general government, banks, and other sectors.

5. *Further by long- or short-term investment* (in the case of other investment and the debt securities component of portfolio investment) *according to the original maturity of the instrument.*

The high-level components of the financial account, along with the capital account, are presented in Table 9. Readers are referred to pages 43–48 in the *BPM5* for the full standard-component listing of the balance of payments.

---

[23]A supplement to the *BPM5* on financial derivatives was issued in 2000.

Regarding the holdings of reserve assets by the monetary authorities, factors other than the transactions in those assets may affect them. For example, the IMF's allocation of SDRs to its member countries increases each country's holdings of reserve assets, but the allocation has no counterpart in economic transactions. Similarly, other factors that are not transactions are the monetization or demonetization of gold by the monetary authorities or the change in the value of reserve assets arising from exchange rate movements. These nontransactional changes in reserve assets are shown as other economic flows.

Surplus or Deficit

In public debate, the expressions *surplus* or *deficit* in the balance of payments are frequently used. They are often left undefined and may have different meanings in different countries. Broadly, a *surplus* refers to a positive balance for a set of transactions (that is, when the sum of the credit entries exceeds the sum of the debit entries), whereas a *deficit* refers to a negative balance of the set of transactions (that is, when the sum of the debit entries exceeds the sum of the credit entries).

At one time IMF staff endeavored to precisely define the concept of *overall surplus* or *deficit*, but it soon became clear that this approach gave rise to a number of difficult borderline cases. More recently, countries have used a more flexible approach, recognizing that sound policy cannot be based on a single figure but must involve analyzing the balance of payments as a whole, in the context of economic developments at home and abroad. For policy purposes, countries now use analytic statements involving several balances. These balances may include the goods and services balance, the current balance, and the financial account balance.

Balance of Payments Presentations

Two types of balance of payments presentations are the *standard presentation* and the *analytic presentation*.

Standard presentation

Table 10 shows a worked example of a balance of payments standard presentation, which includes in summary form the standard components shown in Tables 8 and 9. The table shows the data in a conventional two-column credit and debit format, based on data examples in the *1993 SNA*. The balance of payments framework is fully harmonized with the national

TABLE 10. BALANCE OF PAYMENTS STANDARD PRESENTATION

	Credit	Debit
Current account	**619**	**578**
Goods and services	*540*	*499*
Goods	462	392
Services	78	107
Income	*69*	*40*
Current transfers	*10*	*39*
Capital and financial account		
Capital account	*1*	*4*
Financial account	*50*	*88*
Direct investment abroad	0	3
Direct investment in reporting economy	2	0
Portfolio investment assets	0	20
Portfolio investment liabilities	5	0
Financial derivatives assets	0	0
Financial derivatives liabilities	0	0
Other investment assets	0	64
Other investment liabilities	43	0
Reserve assets	0	1

accounts,[24] and the net lending (+)/net borrowing (−) in the *1993 SNA* is equivalent to the sum of current and capital accounts in the balance of payments.

Analytic presentation

Table 11 provides an example of an *analytic presentation.*[25] Analytic statements strategically regroup the balance of payments standard components to focus on particular analytic issues. In this case, Table 11 rearranges the entries from Table 10 into a single-column format with credits shown as positive entries and debits as negative entries.

The table reclassifies certain entries with reserve assets and introduces various balances. Analysts have derived several balances by distinguishing *above-the-line* components from *below-the-line* components and including a measure of *overall balance* that distinguishes *autonomous transactions*

---

[24]Some minor classification differences exist, including the treatment of financial intermediation services indirectly measured (FISIM).

[25]This is the format used in the analytic statements in the *Balance of Payments Statistics Yearbook* (IMF, various issues) and *International Financial Statistics* (IMF, various issues).

TABLE 11. BALANCE OF PAYMENTS ANALYTIC PRESENTATION

A. Current account balance[1]	**41**
Goods: exports f.o.b.	462
Goods: imports f.o.b.	–392
Balance on goods	*70*
Services: credit	78
Services: debit	–107
Balance on goods and services	*41*
Income: credit	69
Income: debit	–40
Balance on goods, services, and income	*70*
Current transfers: credit	10
Current transfers: debit	–39
B. Capital account balance[1]	**–3**
Capital account: credit	1
Capital account: debit	–4
Total: groups A and B	*38*
C. Financial account balance[1]	**–37**
Direct investment abroad	–3
Direct investment in reporting economy	2
Portfolio investment assets	–20
Portfolio investment liabilities	5
Financial derivatives assets	0
Financial derivatives liabilities	0
Other investment assets	–64
Other investment liabilities	43
Total: groups A through C	*1*
D. Errors and omissions	**0**
Total: groups A through D	*1*
E. Reserves and related items balance	**–1**
Reserve assets	–1
Use of IMF credit and loans	0
Exceptional financing	0

[1]Excludes components that have been classified in group E.

(that is, *total: groups A through D* in the table) from *accommodating transactions* (that is, those that are included in *group E: reserves and related items*). Thus, the table shows reserve assets and selected liabilities as financing the overall surplus or deficit.

The selected liabilities in the table are those that can be incurred—in conjunction with, or as an alternative to, the use of reserve assets to finance payments deficits—or extinguished to absorb surpluses. They consist of *use of IMF credit and loans* and other arrangements (denoted *exceptional financing*) made by the national authorities (or by other sectors fostered by the authorities) to deal with payments imbalances. Exceptional financing transactions range widely from bond issuance, grants received, and debt forgiveness, to temporary accumulation of payments in arrears.

International Investment Position

The *IIP* is the balance sheet of financial assets and liabilities for an economy with respect to the rest of the world. It provides information on the stock of those financial assets and liabilities at the beginning and end of the period; it also describes the changes in those stocks in terms of transactions, revaluations, and other economic flows. Revaluations separately identify price changes for the asset/liability from exchange rate changes.[26] The net IIP—external financial assets minus external liabilities—shows the difference between what an economy owns in other economies in relation to what it owes. The net IIP, combined with the stock of an economy's nonfinancial assets, constitutes the net worth of that economy.[27]

The IIP is classified in the same way as the financial account of the balance of payments. Also, the key concepts guiding the compilation of IIP statistics—residence, valuation, and time of recording—are the same as for the balance of payments and national accounts. The items constituting financial assets and liabilities are financial claims on and liabilities to nonresidents, equity assets and liabilities, financial derivative instruments, monetary gold, and SDRs. The financial instruments making up the assets and liabilities could be grouped according to the functional type of investment—direct investment, portfolio investment, financial derivatives, other investment, and reserve assets. Table 12 provides a worked example of the IIP framework, based on the data examples in the *1993 SNA*.

The IIP provides a picture of the portfolio of external assets and liabilities for an economy at a point in time: this portfolio is normally the result

---

[26]When the domestic currency *depreciates* against the currency of denomination, then the value of the asset/liability denominated in foreign currency will increase in domestic currency terms, and the exchange rate changes will be positive. Conversely, when the domestic currency *appreciates* against the currency of denomination, then the value of the asset/liability denominated in foreign currency will decrease in domestic currency terms, and the exchange rate changes will be negative.

[27]*BPM5*, pages 104–07.

TABLE 12. INTERNATIONAL INVESTMENT POSITION

	Position at Beginning of Year	Transactions	Price and Exchange Rate Changes	Other Adjustments	Position at End of Year
Assets	**573**	**50**	**7**	**0**	**630**
Direct investment abroad	113	2	3	0	118
Portfolio investment	125	5	4	0	134
Financial derivatives	0	0	0	0	0
Other investment	335	42	0	0	377
Reserve assets	0	1	0	0	1
Liabilities	**297**	**88**	**3**	**0**	**388**
Direct investment in reporting economy	3	3	0	0	6
Portfolio investment	77	20	2	0	99
Financial derivatives	0	0	0	0	0
Other investment	217	65	0	0	283

of past external transactions measured according to current market values (current market prices and exchange rates) and other factors (such as write-offs or reclassifications).

A country can use an IIP to analyze the appropriateness of its external asset portfolio against its debt profile. It can also use a set of IIPs for a number of periods to assess developments in the portfolio over time. Indeed, the IIP provides a meaningful basis for countries to analyze rates of return of their external investments. Often, they can use net IIP of an economy to analyze developments and trends in the performance of an economy with the rest of the world. The IIP differs from measures of gross external debt by including information on financial assets and nondebt liabilities (such as equity and financial derivatives).

External Debt Statistics

For measuring and presenting *external debt* statistics, the *External Debt Statistics: Guide for Compilers and Users*, published by the IMF in 2003 (BIS and others, 2003), aims to comprehensively guide users, advising on compiling and analyzing the data. The IMF and other international organizations developed the *Guide* in response to concerns of markets and policymakers to have better data to help assess external vulnerabilities at

**Box 11. Data Template on International Reserves
and Foreign Currency Liquidity**

The data template on international reserves and foreign currency liquidity is designed to integrate the concepts of international reserves and foreign currency liquidity within a single framework. It covers not only the authorities' foreign currency resources on a given date but also inflows and outflows of foreign exchange over a future one-year period. This provides a broader framework for assessing countries' foreign currency liquidity, considered necessary at a time of increasing complexity and importance of such information.

The template provides a comprehensive account of country authorities' foreign currency assets and the drains on such resources resulting from various foreign currency liabilities and commitments of the authorities. It reports the amount and composition of official reserves and other foreign currency assets by the monetary authorities and the central government. It also reports foreign currency obligations of the monetary authorities and central government coming due in the short term, including those related to their financial derivative positions and guarantees extended for quasi-official and private sector borrowing.

To assist countries that are compiling the template to report accurately, the IMF issued in 2001 the *International Reserves and Foreign Currency Liquidity: Guidelines for a Data Template* (Kester, 2001), replacing a provisional 1999 issue (IMF, 1999).

a time when increasing international capital flows are resulting in greater market interdependence.

A previous guide on external debt, published in 1988, used a measure of debt commonly known as disbursed and outstanding debt valued in nominal terms. Largely, this measure reflected the traditional focus on borrowing from banks and government sources, often by the public sector.

For many countries, the growth in the 1990s in cross-border private capital flows led to a need for a broader focus. The *Guide* introduced a comprehensive framework based on the *1993 SNA* for measuring the gross external debt position. Under this framework, gross external debt includes all liabilities (other than equity and financial derivatives) owed to nonresidents. The framework is consistent with the balance of payments and IIP.

Box 12. Foreign Direct Investment Statistics

Direct investment, a category of international investment, reflects the objective of a resident entity in one economy obtaining a lasting interest in an enterprise resident in another economy. The lasting interest implies the existence of a long-term relationship between the direct investor and the enterprise and a significant degree of influence by the investor over the management of the enterprise.

Growing international linkages through direct investment are an important feature of globalization. The integration of capital markets and the consequent rapid growth in direct investment have brought increased scrutiny of the activities of multinational enterprises. In scrutinizing these activities, analysts widely use two sets of statistics:
- Direct investment statistics, which measure cross-border positions and flows between entities in direct investment relationships; and
- Statistics that measure the operations of foreign affiliates of multinational enterprises—such a as sales, employment, and assets—and thus provide a measure of the impact of the direct investment on the economy. These statistics are often referred to as foreign affiliates trade statistics.

The direct investment statistics form components of the balance of payments and IIP. They provide data for balance of payments forecasting, economic surveillance, and vulnerability analysis. To facilitate analysis, countries often extend direct investment statistics to provide geographical information on transactions and positions by partner country and region and to provide breakdowns by industrial sector. Harmonized international statistical guidelines are provided in the *BPM5* and, in more detail, in the *OECD Benchmark Definition of Foreign Direct Investment*, third edition (OECD, 1996).

The priority that individual countries give to compiling data series going beyond gross external debt, presented in the *Guide,* will vary depending on circumstances. However, the *Guide* strongly recommends that countries compile data on the debt-service schedule (the timing and magnitude of future payments) and currency composition of external debt (an indicator of exposure to exchange rate movement). These data reveal essential information on the external vulnerabilities facing an economy.

Similarly, the *Guide* advises on how to measure the net external debt position—gross external debt less external assets in the form of debt instruments. For economies whose private sector is active in financial mar-

Box 13. Coordinated Portfolio Investment Survey

The coordinated portfolio investment survey (CPIS) is an international survey of the holdings of portfolio investment assets. The survey provides data on holdings of equity and debt securities (both short- and long-term) from the perspective of security holders. It brings together data on the type of issue, country of residence of issue, and country of holder. It also contains some information on the sector of holder and currency of issue.

Countries also collect a similar breakdown of securities in the reserve assets of many of the major economies holding reserve assets, and securities of international organizations, but these data are published in aggregate from the asset side.

Because countries provide the data on a bilateral basis, the survey provides information about the counterparty security liabilities of debtor countries, which could use this information to estimate their own outstanding liabilities. It also helps other users understand the magnitude of cross-border exposure of countries. The CPIS complements the IIP data by providing a more detailed view of portfolio investment activity.

To help jurisdictions undertake the survey, the IMF published a *Survey Guide* (*Coordinated Portfolio Investment Survey Guide*; IMF, 1996b) and a second edition of the *Survey Guide* (IMF, 2002a).

kets, the net external debt concept, like the net IIP, is particularly relevant in assessing the sustainability of the external position.[28]

Direct Investment, Portfolio Investment, and International Reserves

Three other data sets complement balance of payments and IIP statistics by providing a more detailed view of activities encompassed within, or linked to, these frameworks. These data sets, described in Boxes 11 (page 58), 12 (page 59), and 13, are the data template on international reserves and foreign currency liquidity, the foreign direct investment statistics, and the coordinated portfolio investment survey.

---

[28]See Chapters 15 and 16 of the *Guide* for a discussion of the analytic uses of external debt data.

IV

Monetary and Financial Statistics

Monetary and financial statistics consist of a comprehensive set of stock and flow data on the financial and nonfinancial assets and liabilities of an economy's financial corporations sector. The financial corporations sector plays an important role in matching units that have net lending surpluses with those that have borrowing requirements. Different types of financial corporations play specific roles, and a wide array of financial instruments exists to meet the complex needs of units active in financial markets. To show financial flows among the units and sectors of an economy and corresponding financial asset and liability positions, specialists have created statistical formats to organize and present the monetary and financial statistics.

Primarily, monetary and financial statistics provide important information on money measures, credit to various sectors, and foreign financial assets and liabilities; in addition, they provide valuable links to government finance and balance of payments statistics. They are often available on a more timely and frequent basis than other sets of macroeconomic data. Even countries that follow inflation targeting and do not establish money or credit growth targets may find monetary and financial statistics useful for information on intersectoral financial relationships and links with the rest of the world. Monetary and financial data are important for formulating and implementing monetary policy and broader types of macroeconomic policy.

The *Monetary and Financial Statistics Manual (MFSM*; IMF, 2000c) provides the methodology for compiling monetary and financial statistics that support these continuing needs. In drafting the *MFSM,* experts carefully harmonized it as much as possible with the *1993 SNA* and other macroeconomic statistical systems. In particular, the *MFSM* incorporates the same criteria as the other systems for residency, definition of institutional sectors, and accounting rules for the identification, timing, and valuation of flows and stocks. Like the other macroeconomic statistics, the *MFSM* encompasses transactions, other economic flows, and stock positions. Thus:

The opening balance sheet

> *plus* transactions in financial assets and liabilities
> *plus* other economic flows

equals the closing balance sheet.

Readers should note that, unlike the other systems, monetary and financial statistics do not directly measure current account transactions. Transactions in goods and services, income, and transfers are reflected in the assets, liabilities, and net worth of the units being measured. According to the *MFSM,* the main transactions and positions being measured relate to financial assets and liabilities, although transactions and positions in nonfinancial assets are also reflected.

Other economic flows include holding gains/losses from changes in market prices and exchange rates, particularly important in monetary and financial statistics, and certain other volume changes, particularly debt write-offs, that may be important in specific units or sectors. The *MFSM* covers stock positions and flows, but many countries, at present, continue to focus data collection and analysis mainly on stock data.

The *MFSM* framework for the monetary statistics embodies two levels of data compilation and presentation. The *first* level aggregates stock and flow data, reported by individual institutional units, into sectoral balance sheets. The balance sheets contain comprehensive data for each financial corporation subsector—the central bank, other depository corporations, and other financial corporations. The *second* level consolidates the data in the sectoral balance sheets into surveys. Countries also use the data in the sectoral balance sheets to compile financial statistics.

In addition, for financial sector surveillance, countries can use the data from the *MFSM* framework to support the construction of the matrix of sectoral balance sheets. For example, to support macroprudential analysis, experts have developed new analytical tools called financial soundness indicators (FSIs; Box 14).

Knowing the concepts of *aggregating, consolidating,* and *netting* macro-economic statistics is particularly useful in understanding monetary and financial statistics. Box 15 sets out these concepts as they apply to collecting and compiling financial statistics, such as flow of funds accounts, within the *1993 SNA* framework. Although for these broader aggregates, experts do not recommend consolidating between sectors and subsectors and netting claims against liabilities, they do consider certain consolidating and

Box 14. Financial Soundness Indicators

Financial soundness indicators (FSIs) are indicators of the current financial health and soundness of entire sectors of financial institutions, as well as the corporate and household sectors—the counterparts of financial institutions. Countries compile the indicators from sectoral data that aggregate and consolidate individual institution data. FSIs also include indicators about the markets in which the financial institutions operate. Aimed at supporting macroprudential analysis, FSIs are to be used in tandem with other tools of such analysis.

The concepts and definitions, as well as sources and techniques for compiling FSIs, are contained in the IMF's *Financial Soundness Indicators: Compilation Guide* (IMF, 2006). To develop this new and coherent methodology for the conceptual framework, the IMF drew selectively from prudential and commercial accounting frameworks (for monitoring individual entities), as well as from macroeconomic statistics frameworks (for monitoring aggregate activity in the economy). The *Guide* distinguishes between two sets of FSIs—core and encouraged. The *core* FSIs, deemed highly relevant in a wide range of countries, cover indicators for the deposit-taking sector. The *encouraged* FSIs, likely to be relevant for some countries, cover the financial and nonfinancial sectors and also include indicators of market liquidity and real estate markets.

netting of positions and flows to be considerably valuable in traditional monetary statistics analysis.

The following sections in this chapter describe (1) the coverage of monetary and financial statistics, (2) financial assets and liabilities, (3) monetary aggregates and depository corporations, (4) the depository corporations survey (DCS), (5) the financial corporations survey (FCS), and (6) flow of funds statistics.

Coverage of Monetary and Financial Statistics

Addressing the coverage of monetary and financial statistics, the *MFSM* identifies three types of financial corporations: the *central bank*, *other depository corporations*, and *other financial corporations*. The central bank and other depository corporations (together, depository corporations) are the institutional focus of monetary statistics; other financial corporations include insurance corporations and pension funds, other financial intermediaries, and financial auxiliaries.

Box 15. Aggregation, Consolidation, and Netting Within the *1993 SNA* Framework

Aggregation refers to summing stock or flow data across all institutional units within a sector or subsector or across all assets or liabilities within a particular category. Aggregating data across the institutional units within a sector or subsector preserves the data on claims and liabilities between the units in that sector or subsector.

For sectors and subsectors, national data compilers aggregate data on financial assets and liabilities into major categories—for example, loans classified by debtor sector and deposits classified by creditor sector. Compilers further aggregate the data to combine major categories of financial assets or liabilities—for example, when combining major categories of monetary assets to form the monetary aggregates or when adding together major categories of claims on various sectors to compile credit aggregates.

Consolidation refers to eliminating stocks and flows occurring between institutional units in a group. Individual institutional units should compile financial flows and stock positions between institutional units but not within an institutional unit. In particular, an institutional unit consisting of a headquarters office and branch offices should compile stock and flow data consolidated across all offices of the institutional unit. For sectors and subsectors, units should not consolidate, as a matter of principle, the flows between institutional units at the elemental level of data reporting and compilation.

Netting refers to specific recommended instances; for example, units should record transactions on a purchases-*less*-sales basis (that is, net acquisition of a specific category of financial assets or liabilities). They should define deposit transactions in a particular category as the amount of new deposits *less* withdrawals during the period. Similarly, units should define securities transactions as the amount of securities purchased *less* the amount redeemed or sold, and loan transactions are defined as the amount of new loans *less* loans repayments, and so forth.

In general, however, units collect and compile the data on a gross basis. In particular, they should *not net* claims on a particular transactor or group of transactors against the liabilities to that transactor or group. For example, a depository corporation might have an outstanding loan to a customer who is also one of its depositors. Compilers should not net the financial corporation's asset (that is, the loan claim) against the liability (that is, the deposit of the borrower).

In exceptional circumstances, regarding claims against liabilities, countries may find it necessary or useful to compile and present data on a net basis for practical reasons. The need to resort to such netting is expected to be relatively rare for most categories of assets and liabilities in the financial corporations sectors of most countries.

The *central bank* is the national financial institution exercising control over key aspects of the financial system. Its activities include issuing currency, managing international reserves, transacting with the IMF, and providing credit to other depository corporations.

Other depository corporations are all resident units engaging primarily in financial intermediation and issuing liabilities included in the national definition of broad money. A measure of money in a given country will depend on the financial instruments available, the financial institutions, and the structure and behavior of financial markets. Thus, it is not possible to specify a precise definition of money applying to all countries. For this reason, it is also not possible to define other depository corporations by the names of institutions. Typically included in depository corporations are all units accepting deposits (demand, time, savings), such as commercial banks, savings banks, building societies, and so forth. However, a unit funded exclusively through the issuance of securities would be classified as a depository corporation if those securities were included in the national definition of broad money in a particular country.

Other financial corporations include insurance corporations and pension funds, other financial intermediaries, and financial auxiliaries. Financial auxiliaries provide services to financial intermediaries and financial markets but do not incur liabilities for the purpose of financial intermediation. For example, security brokers act as agents between buyers and sellers of securities but do not take title to the securities. Other examples of financial auxiliaries are securities exchanges, foreign exchange companies, and units specializing in guarantees.

Among other financial corporations, insurance corporations include those units providing life, accident, health, fire, and other types of insurance to individual units or groups of units. Pension funds are units established to provide retirement benefits for specific groups of employees. Classified as part of general government are social security schemes funded through taxes and controlled by government units that provide retirement and other benefits to members of the community as a whole. Other financial intermediaries cover a very broad range of units that incur liabilities to acquire financial assets but whose liabilities are not included in broad money. These other financial intermediaries may provide credit to other units similar to the credit provided by depository corporations; thus, the classification must be based on the nature of the liabilities.

Financial Assets and Liabilities

As discussed in the introduction to this pamphlet, *financial assets* are a subset of economic assets—entities over which institutional units enforce ownership rights, individually or collectively, and from which they can derive economic benefits by holding or using the assets over a period. Most financial assets originate from financial claims arising from contractual relationships entered into when one institutional unit provides funds to another. Financial assets are therefore financial claims having demonstrable value.

Such contracts, through which asset holders acquire unconditional claims on other institutional units, create creditor/debtor (*asset* and *liability*) relationships with regard to a financial instrument. Exceptions are monetary gold and SDRs—they are financial assets by convention for which there are no corresponding *liabilities.*

Using the *1993 SNA* classification scheme, the *MFSM* classifies financial assets based on two broad criteria: the liquidity of the asset and the legal characteristic underlying the creditor/debtor relationship. The liquidity concept encompasses other more specific characteristics, such as negotiability, transferability, marketability, and convertibility.

Other financial assets within the framework of monetary and financial statistics and as defined in the introduction are currency and deposits, securities other than shares, loans, shares and other equity, insurance technical reserves, financial derivatives, and other accounts receivable/payable.

Readers should note that contractual financial arrangements that do not create unconditional claims on other institutional units, such as guarantees of payment by third parties or lines of credit, are normally referred to as contingencies and are excluded from the monetary and financial statistics.[29]

Monetary Aggregates and Depository Corporations

No single definition of money can be applied to all countries. What is considered to be money reflects a range of issues, including the financial instruments available in a country, the types of financial institutions, and the level of development of financial markets. The *MFSM*, therefore, does not recommend a specific measure or measures of money but rather

---

[29]Even though excluded from the monetary and financial statistics, data on contingencies should be reported as memorandum items.

describes the issues that a country should take into account in deriving money measures.

The *MFSM* focuses on a country's developing *broad money* measures. Narrow money measures include instruments used directly for making transactions, whereas broad money aggregates include instruments that serve a range of purposes, including making transactions, serving as a store of value, providing income in the form of interest, and so forth. Few countries focus solely on narrow money measures, primarily because other instruments may be substituted quite easily for the transaction instruments.

In defining money measures, countries specify three dimensions: which *instruments* to include, who to include as *money holders*, and which institutions to include as *money issuers*, as shown in the following paragraphs.

First, the *instruments* countries may include in money measures are currency, deposits, and securities other than shares. Countries always include national currency and transferable deposits in money measures, and most countries also include other deposits, unless these deposits are so highly restricted that they do not serve the purposes of money. Some countries include securities other than shares in money measures, when the securities are close substitutes for deposits. For example, negotiable certificates of deposit issued by financial institutions may have many of the same characteristics as deposits accepted by these institutions. Other categories of financial assets are rarely included in money measures.

Second, in defining a measure of money, countries also must specify who to include as *holders* of monetary instruments. Most countries define money holders to include all resident sectors except depository corporations and central government. Thus, money holders are state and local governments, nonfinancial corporations, financial corporations other than depository corporations, households, and nonprofit institutions serving households (NPISH).

Third, *money issuers* include all financial corporations having as liabilities the financial instruments considered to have monetary characteristics. This group of institutions will include the central bank (generally the issuer of currency), commercial and other banks that accept transferable deposits, units that accept other types of deposits (savings banks, building societies, and so forth), and units that issue short-term securities considered by holders to be close substitutes for deposits. It is not possible to identify a money issuer by the name of the institution. For example, "finance companies" accept deposits in some countries, while in others, controlling institutions fund finance companies directly.

Many countries specify a range of money measures from M1 (currency and transferable deposits) through M2, M3, and so forth. The aggregates differ according to the degree of "moneyness" of the assets included. The higher-ordered monetary aggregates (MAs) include a broader range of monetary instruments, such as foreign-currency-denominated deposits and deposits of longer maturities or those with greater restrictions on conversion into transactions money.

By definition, depository corporations include all financial corporations that issue liabilities included in the national definition of broad money.

Depository Corporations Survey

When assessing monetary statistics, analysts use mainly the *DCS*, which presents depository corporations' broad money liabilities. This section outlines how countries prepare and use a DCS—collecting the monetary and financial statistics, compiling the statistics in balance sheets, and making analytical presentations in monetary surveys, specifically the DCS.

For *collecting* monetary and financial statistics, the *MFSM* recommends countries collect the data in a way that identifies the *types of financial instruments* in the data and, for each instrument, the *positions* with main sectors and subsectors of the economy. That is, they need to identify which units the financial corporations have claims on and which units have claims on the financial corporations. To identify the financial instruments, countries can use an eight-category classification scheme (see Box 2), and to identify units, they can use the institutional sector and subsector description in Chapter 2 of the *MFSM*.

For *compiling* the data from the reporting institutions, the *MFSM* recommends countries use *sectoral balance sheets*. Sectoral balance sheets organize data by categories of assets and liabilities, by resident and nonresident categories, and by appropriate breakdown of the resident sectors—thereby allowing staff to directly prepare presentations for policy and analytical purposes.

The *main analytical presentations* recommended by the *MFSM* are *monetary surveys*—consolidated sectoral balance sheets for one or more subsectors of the financial corporations sector. Surveys cover specific subsectors like the central bank, other depository corporations, and other financial corporations. Surveys also consolidate subsectors. Thus, a *DCS* consolidates the surveys for the central bank and other depository corporations. And the *FCS* (discussed in the next section) consolidates the depository corporations survey and the other financial corporations survey.

The main survey that analysts use to assess monetary statistics is the *DCS*, which relates depository corporations' broad money liabilities to their foreign assets and liabilities, their net claims on central government, and their claims on other resident sectors. Hence, the DCS links the monetary statistics to the balance of payments and government finance statistics (GFS), respectively, as well as to other sectors.

The DCS is presented in the following general format:[30]

> Assets
>> Net foreign assets
>> Domestic claims
>>> Net claims on central government
>>> Credit to other resident sectors
> Liabilities
>> Broad money
>>> Currency outside depository corporations
>>> Transferable deposits
>>> Other deposits
>>> Securities other than shares
>> Other liabilities (by instrument)
>> Other items (net)

Under *assets*, the DCS identifies claims on and liabilities to nonresidents, presenting these as *net foreign assets*. This provides a direct link to the operations of depository corporations affecting the balance of payments. *Domestic claims* may be broken down according to a country's specific structure and analytical needs, thereby providing the most useful measures of credit.[31] Most countries identify separately *net credit to central government*, permitting a measure of central government financing provided by

---

[30]All of the surveys follow the same basic analytical structure.

[31]Unlike the central government sector, claims on other domestic sectors are presented on a gross basis. Government deposits are excluded from broad money because the rationale for managing these deposits, influenced by policy considerations, is different from the one guiding the managing of the deposits of other sectors of the economy, including nonfinancial public enterprises. Therefore, claims on central government are presented on a net basis.

depository corporations. *Other domestic sectors* may be broken down by state and local government, public and private corporations, households, nonprofit institutions, and any other mix that is thought appropriate. Many countries also classify credit according to whether the credit is provided to businesses or consumers.

Under *liabilities*, the DCS breaks down broad money by the type of financial instrument in the general framework. In a presentation, countries will often group these instruments into different money measures, proceeding from currency and transferable deposits (M1) to broader measures. The specific measures will depend on the purpose of the analysis and the reliability of the relationship between specific money measures and intermediate or final target variables in the economy.

How Does the Depository Corporations Survey Presentation Facilitate Monetary Analysis?

This DCS presentation facilitates standard approaches to monetary analysis that identify money and factors affecting changes in money through the following identity:

$$M = NFA + NCG + CORS - OIN,$$

where M is the country-specific measure of broad money, NFA (net foreign assets) is the net position with nonresidents (the balance of payments effect), NCG is net claims on central government, $CORS$ is credit to other resident sectors, and OIN is the net position of all other items.

Because monetary surveys are based on balance sheet data, their components represent stock data. For analytical purposes, countries can express the identity as changes (Δ) during a period, say, one month or one year:

$$\Delta M = \Delta NFA + \Delta NCG + \Delta CORS - \Delta OIN.$$

Table 13 presents an example of changes in the DCS. It includes hypothetical data entries based on the data examples in the *1993 SNA*.[32]

---

[32]However, there is no direct link to the *1993 SNA* data examples for several reasons. First, in the financial accounts of the *1993 SNA* all sectors may hold currency and deposits, whereas in the DCS money issuers (central bank and other depository corporations) do not hold them. Second, the *1993 SNA* financial account of a sector is not consolidated, whereas one of the principles for constructing the DCS is the consolidation of accounts between institutional units within a sector.

TABLE 13. DEPOSITORY CORPORATIONS SURVEY
(Annual changes)

Net foreign assets	23	**Broad money**	105
Monetary gold and SDRs	...	Currency	23
Foreign currency	...	Deposits	82
Deposits	...	Securities other than shares	0
Net credit to central government	16	**Other items, net**	63
Credit to central government	...		
Government deposits	...		
Credit to other resident sectors	129		

Countries that consider the monetary base or reserve money to be an important analytical or policy variable focus on the *central bank survey*. They present the central bank survey in the same format as the depository corporations survey, with the monetary base replacing broad money. Definitions of *monetary base* differ across countries but invariably include currency in circulation and deposits of other depository corporations in the central bank. Some countries have a broader definition, including also deposits of all other resident sectors, except central government, in the central bank. The *MFSM* does not make a specific recommendation about the composition of the monetary base.

Financial Corporations Survey

Many countries have found that changes in the structure of the financial markets, the roles of financial institutions, and the mix of financial instruments available have lessened the usefulness of focusing on specific measures of money. In that case, the *FCS* serves to analyze financial positions for the complete financial sector. This survey is particularly useful in analyzing the credit provided by all financial intermediaries.

The relevance of the FCS has increased as activities by other financial corporations have expanded, in particular by insurance corporations and pension funds. These institutions can manage financial assets and have financial liabilities constituting a significant proportion of the financial assets and liabilities of the other depository corporations sector.

In the same way that countries construct a DCS, they can construct an FCS, which analytically presents the financial corporations sector's claims

71

on, and liabilities to, all other domestic sectors and nonresidents. Unlike the DCS, the FCS is not structured around the concept of broad money. Moreover, in the liability section, the FCS presents as a separate item *insurance technical reserves*, to highlight the importance of these liabilities within the total liabilities.

Flow of Funds Statistics

In many countries, the development of financial markets has reduced the relative importance of financial intermediaries in providing credit and other financial services. For example, corporations that traditionally borrowed from banks may now meet their financing needs by issuing securities on the financial market and obtaining their financing from a mix of domestic and foreign lenders. If analyzing these developments is considered important, a country may develop a broader basis for financial analysis called *financial accounts* or *flow of funds*. A flow of funds measures all the important financial relationships in an economy and between an economy and the rest of the world. The *MFSM* provides guidance in establishing flow of funds accounts, drawing from the *1993 SNA*.

The national accounts' discussion earlier showed how the financial account for an economy describes the economy's net lending/borrowing transactions with the rest of the world, and the financial instruments involved. If the economy has more savings and capital transfers than it does capital formation, then the account reflects the surplus in *net lending* to the rest of the world. Conversely, if it has less savings and capital transfers than capital formation, the deficit is financed by *net borrowing* from the rest of the world. Primarily, the national account's net lending/borrowing (NL/B) by an economy should be identical to the information presented in the financial account of the balance of payments.

The earlier discussion also noted that countries can compile the sequence of accounts for each domestic sector of the economy. Table 14 gives the financial account from the *1993 SNA* by sector. It provides useful information on how each domestic sector contributes to the overall NL/B of the economy.

The data in Table 14 from the *1993 SNA* show an economy that is a net lender to the rest of the world (by 38 units). The sectoral data are fairly typical in that they show that the nonfinancial corporations and general government sectors are net borrowers, and households are net lenders. Al-

TABLE 14. FINANCIAL ACCOUNTS (*1993 SNA*) BY SECTOR

	Nonfinancial Corporations	Financial Corporations	General Government	Households	NPISH	Total Economy
Net acquisitions of financial assets	**71**	**237**	**120**	**181**	**32**	**641**
F.1 Monetary gold and SDRs		−1				−1
F.2 Currency and deposits	17	15	7	68	12	119
F.3 Securities other than shares	18	53	26	29	12	138
F.4 Loans	27	167	45	5		244
F.5 Shares and other equity	2	3	36	3		44
F.6 Insurance technical reserves				36		36
F.7 Financial derivatives	0	0	0	0	0	0
F.8 Other accounts receivable	7		6	40	8	61
Net incurrence of liabilities	**140**	**232**	**170**	**33**	**28**	**603**
F.2 Currency and deposits		130	2			132
F.3 Securities other than shares	6	53	64			123
F.4 Loans	71		94	28	24	217
F.5 Shares and other equity	26	13			4	43
F.6 Insurance technical reserves		36				36
F.7 Financial derivatives	0	0	0	0	0	0
F.8 Other accounts payable	37		10	5		52
B.9 Net lending (+)/net borrowing (−)	**−69**	**5**	**−50**	**148**	**4**	**38**

though the financial corporations sector has a large volume of transactions in financial assets and liabilities, the sector typically is neither an overall net borrower nor a net lender.

The sectoral table also shows the financial instruments used to effect the net lending or borrowing. For example, the nonfinancial corporations sector acquires a spread of financial assets and incurs liabilities mainly in the form of loans (71) and shares and other equity (26). On the other hand, the financial corporations sector acquires a large part of its assets in the form of loans (167) and incurs equivalent liabilities largely in the form of currency and deposits (130) and securities other than shares (53). The large value of transactions in both financial assets and liabilities by the financial corporations sector reflects its role in financial intermediation.

Although this table presents a good deal of useful information, it does not answer the question of who is financing whom. For a full understanding of financial flows and the role they play in the economy, users need more detail on the relationships among the sectors involved. For example, from Table 14, users can see that the government has incurred liabilities in the form of securities other than shares (64) and loans (94), but they cannot determine whether the borrowing has taken place domestically or abroad. They can answer this question only by having more details on the counterparty to the transaction.[33] The need for more detailed sectoral data is particularly important when analysts assess the role of financial intermediaries.

This more detailed presentation of financial transactions by instrument and counterparty sector is known as *detailed flow of funds accounting*. This presentation cross-classifies financial assets acquired by each sector by instrument and the counterpart debtor sector. It also cross-classifies liabilities incurred by each sector by instrument and counterpart creditor sector. The level of sectoral detail presented depends on the needs of the country concerned. However, typically a detailed flow of funds presents data for each sector of the economy—with the financial corporations sector broken into subsectors (central bank, other depository corporations, other financial corporations, financial auxiliaries, and insurance corporations

---

[33]The macroeconomic statistical standards include tables and classifications that provide some of this additional information. For example, the classification of monetary statistics and the balance of payments identifies the domestic counterparty sector, and the *GFSM 2001* includes a table (Table 9.2) that classifies financial transactions by sector.

and pension funds)—allowing analysts to better assess the financial flows. This presentation also gives data for the rest of the world, as if it were an institutional sector. The interlocking row and column constraints within the matrix are an important check on the consistency of the data compilation, considerably increasing the data's usefulness for analysts.

Countries may also complement the detailed flow of funds statistics with data on the stocks of financial assets and liabilities cross-classified by sector and instrument. As described in the *MFSM* (Chapter 8), the entire set of stock and flow data, including not only the transactions (flow of funds) but also other flows, are referred to as financial statistics.

V
Government Finance Statistics

Economists and statisticians have long found it useful to separate the activities of government from those of the rest of the economy because the powers, motivation, and functions of government differ from those of other sectors. Governments have powers to raise taxes and other compulsory levies and to pass laws affecting the behavior of other economic units. They focus on public policy considerations rather than on profit maximization. The principal economic functions of *general government* are

1. To provide goods and services to the community on a nonmarket basis, either for collective consumption (such as public administration, defense, and law enforcement) or individual consumption (education, health, housing, and cultural services); and
2. To redistribute income and wealth by means of transfer payments (taxes and social benefits).

When considering general government statistics, economists also look at the *broader public sector,* because governments often fulfill their public policy objectives through operating public enterprises (for example, railways, airlines, public utilities, and public financial corporations). A government may do so by requiring a corporation to service areas of the economy that would not be otherwise covered and by charging subsidized prices, including lending at low interest rates. As a result, the public corporation operates with a reduced profit or at a loss. Such public policy operations are known as quasi-fiscal activity.

For compiling and analyzing general government and public sector statistics, the *Government Finance Statistics Manual 2001* (*GFSM 2001*; IMF, 2001) provides a comprehensive framework. To a very large extent,[34] it has been harmonized with the *1993 SNA* (Box 16).

The following sections discuss the (1) coverage of general government, (2) basis of recording, (3) analytic framework, and (4) major *GFSM 2001* classifications.

---

[34]The *GFSM 2001* has more features that differ from the *1993 SNA* than any of the other macroeconomic statistical systems. The relationship between the two systems is spelled out in detail in Box 16.

Coverage of General Government

As with the other macroeconomic statistics, the coverage of the *general government* sector is based on classifying resident institutional units. The first criterion for national data compilers to use for sectorizing government units is "control"—if the government controls the unit, compilers classify it as within the public sector; otherwise it is a private sector unit.

Next, compilers classify the public sector units into the general government sector or the *public corporations sector*, on the basis of how the units' output is financed. If the unit primarily sells goods and services at economically significant prices, it is a market producer, and it is classified as a (financial or nonfinancial) public corporation. If the unit does not sell most of its output at economically significant prices, it is a nonmarket producer of goods and services, and it should be classified as part of the general government sector.

Fundamentally, the general government sector covers all institutional units at the central government, state government, and local government levels. It also covers administrative units (budgetary and extrabudgetary), social security funds, and nonmarket nonprofit institutions controlled and mainly financed by government. Therefore, included in the general government sector are such institutional units as extrabudgetary funds, nonprofit institutions controlled by government, and public entities that, although legally having corporation status, do not sell their output at economically significant prices.

Basis of Recording

While governments have used *cash transactions* as the basis of recording government finance statistics, they have become increasingly concerned about the wider resource implications of fiscal actions. Traditionally, governments have kept their accounts on a cash basis. This tradition is reflected in the analytical framework of the 1986 edition of *A Manual on Government Finance Statistics* (*GFSM 1986*; IMF, 1986). The inclusion of only cash revenues and expenditures has the advantage of focusing governments' attention on their *liquidity constraint*, which they viewed traditionally as the most important policy issue. However, as the sole basis for assessing fiscal policy, the use of cash transaction recording has brought increasing dissatisfaction (Box 17).[35] As governments have become less constrained by liquidity in carrying out fiscal policy, they have become

---

[35]Some of the key issues involved in moving from the *GFSM 1986* to *GFSM 2001* are discussed in Box 17.

Box 16. Relationship Between the *GFSM 2001* and the *1993 SNA*

General

The *Government Finance Statistics Manual 2001 (GFSM 2001*; IMF, 2001) and the *1993 SNA* are harmonized to a very large extent. The overall structure and the definition of units are the same in both (the overall structure signifying the recording of full balance sheets and flows; the definition of units distinguishing between transactions, holding gains, and other changes in volume). The classification of sectors and functions are identical, and the classification of transactions is very close. The accounting conventions are identical in both systems.

The main specifics of government finance statistics (GFS) differences are the following:

- The focus is on areas of prime importance to fiscal analysis. This implies, among other things, that the GFS do not include a production account.
- The GFS have fewer core balances than the *1993 SNA*, defining only those essential for fiscal analysis. However, the GFS identify several supplementary analytical balances.
- The GFS break down several transaction categories in greater detail than in the *1993 SNA*, and the classification criteria may also differ in some cases.
- In the GFS, tables specify the sources and uses of cash.
- The GFS emphasize the public sector more than the *1993 SNA* does.
- The GFS emphasize consolidated statements more than the *1993 SNA* does.

Detail

The GFS and the *1993 SNA* differ in quite a number of other respects. They have different backgrounds, as listed below.

Differences that are simplifications or the consequences of simplifications

- In the GFS, inputs for own-account capital formation are not distinguished by type (such as use of goods and services, compensation of employees, and consumption of fixed capital).
- In the GFS, the value of social benefits excludes goods and services produced by government units themselves. This is also the case for transfers of individual nonmarket goods and services to households.
- The GFS treat some in-kind transactions as if they were made in cash, followed by a sale. This applies only to goods or services produced by government itself. Such imputations are made for (1) in-kind wages to government employees; (2) in-kind social benefits provided by government employer

increasingly concerned about the wider resource implications of fiscal actions in addition to their financing. Cash transactions do not adequately record either the timing of the policy action or the impact of these decisions on the economy.

schemes; (3) in-kind grants to other government units and international organizations; and (4) in-kind compensation for damage to property or personal injury, or settlement of an insurance claim.

- The GFS do not adjust interest flows for financial intermediation services indirectly measured (FISIM).
- The GFS do not break down gross non-life-insurance premiums into insurance services and net premiums.
- For employer social insurance schemes that provide retirement benefits, the GFS do not record social contributions (whether actual, imputed, or supplementary) in government revenue. Similarly, the GFS do not record pensions paid as government expense. In the case of unfunded pension schemes, the GFS record these receivables and payables in the balance sheet of the government under insurance technical reserves.
- The GFS do not make imputations for reinvested earnings on direct foreign investment.

Differences that are theoretical improvements

- The GFS treat defined-benefit retirement schemes that are unfunded in a theoretically more adequate way than the *1993 SNA* does. This has various consequences. Where the *1993 SNA* balance sheets record only actual available reserves under the item *insurance technical reserves*, the GFS record the present value of the schemes' pension obligations. Contributions to the schemes reflect payments made in the *1993 SNA*, but in the GFS they also reflect the increase in promised future benefits in the GFS balance sheets. As for property income attributed to insurance policyholders, the *1993 SNA* records the income earned on the reserves held by the schemes. The GFS record instead the increase in pension liabilities that results from the passage of time.

Other

- Whereas the *1993 SNA* records certain flows as taxes paid by general government units, the GFS classify them as miscellaneous other expense in the accounts of individual units and eliminates them in consolidation for the general government sector.
- Whereas the *1993 SNA* records certain flows as subsidies paid to general government units, the GFS classify them as grants.

The *GFSM 2001* extends the cash-based analytical framework by emphasizing the recording of data on an *accrual* basis. That is, it recommends that government accountants record an economic event when economic value

Box 17. Moving from *GFSM 1986* to *GFSM 2001*

Many countries currently compile and present their government finance statistics on a cash basis, using either the framework of *A Manual on Government Finance Statistics 1986* (*GFSM 1986*; IMF, 1986) or their own national frameworks. The definitions used in the *GFSM 1986* to distinguish revenue, expenditure, and financing result in changes in the overall balance that do not properly convey the economic impact of certain fiscal operations. Focusing attention on the government's liquidity position, the *GFSM 1986* framework does not adequately capture the economic activity of government, either in terms of the timing of policy actions or its impact on the economy. Moreover, from an operational standpoint, the *GFSM 1986* lacks an explicit linkage between flows and stocks, which is important for measuring fiscal sustainability. It is important, therefore, that steps be taken to implement the comprehensive framework of the *Government Finance Statistics Manual 2001* (*GFSM 2001*; IMF, 2001).

Implementation of the *GFSM 2001* involves three distinct sets of actions that can be initiated simultaneously but, depending on the relative complexities involved, will be accomplished with different time horizons. These actions are

1. Changing the presentation of the existing data (near term),
2. Improving data reporting (medium term), and
3. Fully implementing accrual reporting and the associated underlying systems (long term).

Of these actions, adopting the *GFSM 2001* presentational format is the easiest to conduct. It essentially involves reclassifying existing fiscal data in the appropriate analytical framework. This activity would require few resources and can be accomplished relatively quickly.

The second action—reporting according to the *GFSM 2001* framework—poses more of a challenge and could be constrained by a lack of statistical capacity. Close collaboration between the national authorities and IMF staff could be required to develop this capacity through training. This could take considerable time.

The third action—full implementation of the *GFSM 2001*—is only achieved with introducing an accounting system based on accrual principles and a modern public expenditure management framework. This would ensure classification systems that are capable of supporting statistical reporting compliant with the *GFSM 2001* framework. Accomplishing this action is a major task for most countries, requiring careful planning and management to avoid disrupting the flow of fiscal statistics. To effectively manage the constraints to implementation at every stage, countries should develop a migration strategy for implementing *GFSM 2001* tailored to institutional capacity.

is created, transformed, exchanged, transferred, or extinguished—not just when the cash flow takes place. This gives a comprehensive picture of government activity, by allowing for the recording of noncash transactions (such as barter or in-kind transfers), internal transactions, other economic flows, the accrual of interest on discounted securities, and any payment arrears.

Warranting special mention is the recording of tax revenue on an accrual basis. The *GFSM 2001* requires accountants to record as revenue only those taxes that countries can reasonably expect to collect. Over time, a close relationship should develop between the accrual recording of tax revenue and the cash received.

Analytical Framework

For its analytical framework, the *GFSM 2001* supports the balance sheet approach (BSA) to analyzing economic policy—bringing together stocks and flows in a transparent and consistent framework. Table 15 illustrates the features of this approach. By presenting fiscal data in an integrated framework, it enables analysts to assess fiscal sustainability—that is, to evaluate how net worth evolves through a series of balance sheets. Moreover, the *GFSM 2001* framework yields of government saving, investment, and consumption are largely harmonized with the national accounts framework.

The *GFSM 2001* framework is composed of summary tables—similar to business financial accounting reports—comprising an operating statement, a balance sheet, and a cash statement. As illustrated in Table 15, the framework consists of four analytic statements: the statement of government operations, the statement of other economic flows, the balance sheet, and the statement of sources and uses of cash (not shown here). Within the tables are the four main balances of the system—four core fiscal indicators—the *net operating balance*, *net lending/borrowing*, and *net worth*, plus the *cash surplus/deficit* (not shown here).

In addition to identifying the main balances of the system, the *GFSM 2001* identifies other analytic measures of potential interest to analysts. These include the *overall primary balance*—adding back the interest expense to the overall fiscal balance to give a measure of the outcome from government's discretionary activities—and the *gross debt position*— measuring the stock of all debt liabilities, as defined in the *GFSM 2001*

TABLE **15.** *GFSM 2001* ANALYTICAL FRAMEWORK

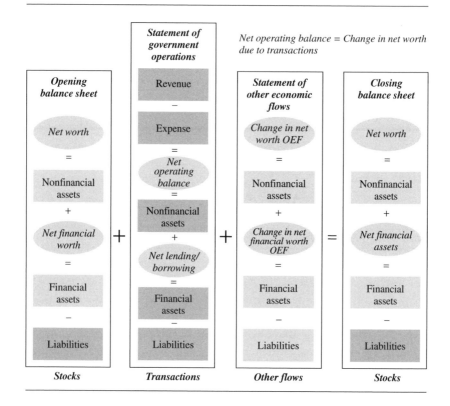

(that is, all liabilities except shares and other equity, and financial derivatives; Box 18).[36]

GFSM 2001 Analytic Statements

Of the four analytic statements of the *GFSM 2001* framework, three are based on accrual data for transactions, other economic flows, and balance sheets, while the fourth is cash-based, as follows:

1. The *statement of government operations* (Table 16) summarizes all transactions by general government units and derives the important

---

[36]This concept, applied to both the general government and public corporations, is used in the measurement of *public sector debt* (see Box 18).

TABLE 16. STATEMENT OF GOVERNMENT OPERATIONS

1. Revenue
  1.1 Taxes
  1.2 Social contributions
  1.3 Grants
  1.4 Other revenue

2. Expense
  2.1 Compensation of employees
  2.2 Use of goods and services
  2.3 Consumption of fixed capital
  2.4 Interest
  2.5 Subsidies
  2.6 Grants
  2.7 Social benefits
  2.8 Other expense

Net operating balance (NOB) (1 minus 2)

3.1 Net acquisition of nonfinancial assets
  3.1.1 Fixed assets
  3.1.2 Inventories
  3.1.3 Valuables
  3.1.4 Nonproduced assets

Net lending/borrowing (NOB minus 3.1)

3.2 Net acquisition of financial assets
  3.2.1 Domestic
  3.2.2 Foreign

3.3 Net incurrence of liabilities
  3.3.1 Domestic
  3.3.2 Foreign

---

analytic balances of *net operating balance* and *net lending/borrowing* (NL/B) from the following information.

The *net operating balance* summarizes the change in net worth owing to government transactions and is ultimately a measure of the sustainability of government policies affecting revenue and expense. It is conceptually equivalent to the national accounting concept of savings plus capital transfers. If the balance is positive, it indicates the government has generated surplus revenue from its current operations, resulting in an increase in its net worth. The government may use this surplus revenue to acquire assets and/or decrease liabilities. If the balance is negative, it indicates that government current

83

Box 18. Public Sector Debt

The public sector debt concepts, definitions, and classifications in the *Government Finance Statistics Manual 2001* (*GFSM 2001*; IMF, 2001) are broadly consistent with those prescribed in *External Debt Statistics: Guide for Compilers and Users* (IMF, 2003; the *Guide*) and the *1993 SNA*. Debt is a subset of liabilities, and according to the *GFSM 2001* (page 129), public sector debt "consists of all liabilities that require payments of interest and/or principal by the debtor to the creditor at a date or dates in the future." Thus, all liabilities of public sector units are debt instruments—except for shares and other equity and financial derivatives, because they do not require payments of interest and/or principal. The *GFSM 2001* recommends valuing these debt instruments at current market values, except for loans, which are normally valued at nominal prices. (The *Guide* recommends valuing tradable debt investments at nominal prices as well as market prices.) Contingent claims on the public sector are not recognized as liabilities in their balance sheets but may be reported as memorandum items.

Total debt instruments issued by public sector units comprise "gross public debt." At the same time, the public sector can hold, as financial assets, the debt instruments issued by institutional units outside the public sector. Then the public sector's net position on debt instruments (that is, assets minus liabilities) constitutes the "net public debt." The public sector's net position (net worth),

operations have fallen short, necessitating the incurrence of liabilities or liquidation of assets to finance the shortfall.

Subtracting the net acquisition of nonfinancial assets from the net operating balance gives a second balance, *NL/B*. NL(+)/B(−) is a summary measure indicating, in essence, the extent to which government is either putting financial resources at the disposal of other sectors in the economy or using the financial resources generated by other sectors. Readers may therefore view the balance as an indicator of the financial impact of government activity on the rest of the economy. It is conceptually equivalent to the national accounting concept of NL/B.

In other words, it may be said that the *net operating balance* focuses on the "activity" side (by considering transactions in revenue and expense), whereas *NL/B* focuses on the "financing" side (by considering transactions in financial assets and liabilities).

over time, is an indicator of the sustainability of government policies. In compiling the balance sheet for the public sector, national compilers should consolidate counterpart claims and liabilities among public sector units with respect to debt instruments (that is, intrapublic sector holdings of debt instruments)—thus excluding them from the gross and/or net public sector debt.

Governments seek to ensure that public debt is sustainable, in the context of broader policy objectives, and that the debt can be serviced under a wide range of macroeconomic circumstances. In this regard, not only the level but the composition of public debt becomes relevant. Vulnerability and sustainability analyses require accurate and timely data on the composition of the public debt in terms of financial instruments, currency composition, residency, and maturity structure. Although the *GFSM 2001* framework prescribes the breakdown of assets and liabilities by residency and instrument, compilers can usefully supplement it with information on currency composition and maturity.

The international statistical community is making efforts to further improve the analytical usefulness of public debt data. A draft public sector debt template, as well as general guidelines for reporting data, is available on the IMF's website at http://www.imf.org/external/pubs/ft/gfs/manual/comp.htm. The template's framework is designed to cover all institutional units within the public sector, covering data for domestic and external debt.

The *statement of other economic flows* presents information on changes in *net worth* arising from economic flows other than transactions. Economists classify these flows as either changes in prices (revaluations) or changes in the volume of assets and liabilities.

2. The *balance sheet* represents the stocks of assets, liabilities, and *net worth* at the beginning and the end of the accounting period.

3. The *statement of sources and uses of cash* (not illustrated here) shows purely cash flows associated with revenue and expense transactions and transactions in nonfinancial assets, which yields the *cash surplus/deficit*. Adding cash flow transactions in financial assets (other than cash) and liabilities to the cash surplus/deficit gives *net change in the stock of cash*.

Tables 17 and 18 summarize some worked examples for the *GFSM 2001* framework, based on data examples in the *1993 SNA*. They highlight

TABLE 17. STATEMENT OF GENERAL GOVERNMENT OPERATIONS

Revenue	**1,046**
Taxes	450
Social contributions[1]	268
Grants[2]	1
Other revenue[3]	327
Expense	**1,084**
Compensation of employees[4]	140
Use of goods and services[4]	252
Consumption of fixed capital[4]	30
Interest	35
Subsidies	44
Grants[2]	58
Social benefits[1]	451
Other expense	74
Net operating balance	**–38**
Net acquisition of nonfinancial assets	**12**
Fixed assets (capital formation)[4]	5
Inventories	0
Valuables	3
Nonproduced nonfinancial assets	4
Net lending/borrowing	**–50**
Transactions in financial assets and liabilities (financing)	**50**
Net acquisition of financial assets	120
Net incurrence of liabilities[1]	170

[1]Assuming no nonautonomous government employee pension fund is included in general government.
[2]Presented after consolidation and including capital grants.
[3]Includes output adjusted for collective consumption.
[4]Assuming no own-account capital formation.

the structure, key elements, and balances (except for the sources and uses of cash) needed for fiscal analysis and policy.

Major *GFSM 2001* Classifications

This section outlines the three major classifications of the *GFSM 2001*: (1) *economic*, identifying the types of outlays governments incur; (2) *functional*, identifying the purpose for which governments undertake the outlays; and (3) *counterparty*, identifying the counterparty sectors.

TABLE 18. INTEGRATED BALANCE SHEET FOR GENERAL GOVERNMENT

	Opening Balance Sheet	Transactions	Holding Gains and Losses	Other Volume Changes	Closing Balance Sheet
NET WORTH	1,300	–38	37	2	1,301
Nonfinancial assets	1,591	12	43	0	1,646
Fixed assets	913	5	18	–3	933
Inventories	47	0	1	0	48
Valuables	41	3	1	0	45
Nonproduced assets	590	4	23	3	620
Tangible nonproduced assets	578	4	23	3	608
Intangible nonproduced assets	12	0	0	0	12
Financial assets	396	120	1	1	518
Domestic and foreign	316	120	0	1	437
Currency and deposits	150	7	0	0	157
Securities other than shares	0	26	0	3	29
Loans	115	45	0	0	160
Shares and other equity	12	36	0	–2	46
Insurance technical reserves	20	0	0	0	20
Financial derivatives	0	0	0	0	0
Other accounts receivable	19	6	0	0	25
Monetary gold and SDRs	80	0	1	0	81
Liabilities	687	170	7	–1	863
Domestic and foreign	687	170	7	–1	863
Currency and deposits	102	2	0	0	104
Securities other than shares	212	64	7	0	283
Loans	328	94	0	–1	421
Shares and other equity	4	0	0	0	4
Insurance technical reserves	19	0	0	0	19
Financial derivatives	0	0	0	0	0
Other accounts payable	22	10	0	0	32

Economic Classification

The *statement of government operations* presents government activity using what is known as an "economic" classification. The statement presents information based on the type of revenue, expense, nonfinancial asset, and financial instrument:

- *Revenue* identifies separately *tax revenue*, forming the dominant share of revenue for most governments; *social contributions*, consisting of receipts from employers or employees that secure employees' entitlements to future social benefits; *grants*, equaling noncompulsory transfers from other government units or international organizations; and *other revenue*, comprising property income, sales of goods and services, and miscellaneous revenue.
- *Expense* identifies separately *compensation of employees*, consisting of the government's labor cost; *use of goods and services*, equaling its cost of materials and services used in production; *consumption of fixed capital*, comprising its cost of using of fixed assets;[37] *interest*, its cost of borrowing; transfers in the form of *subsidies, grants, and social benefits*; and finally, *other expense*, covering all expense transactions not covered elsewhere.
- Transactions in *nonfinancial assets* identify separately the acquisition and disposal of *fixed assets, inventories, valuables*, and *nonproduced assets*.
- Transactions in *financial assets and liabilities* identify the transactions in financing, classified by the instrument involved (for example, loan, deposit, currency, and so forth).

The *balance sheets* and *statement of other economic flows* also use the economic classification of nonfinancial assets and use the type of instrument to classify financial assets and liabilities.

Functional Classification

The economic classification informs users on the type of outlay incurred by the government, but many users are also interested in the purpose for which the outlay was undertaken. The *GFSM 2001* framework satisfies this

---

[37]The *GFSM 2001* defines consumption of fixed capital as the decline in the value of the stock of fixed assets during the accounting period as a result of physical deterioration, normal obsolescence, and accidental damage. This definition is consistent with the national accounts.

interest by applying a functional classification. The *GFSM 2001* framework applies the *Classification of the Functions of Government* (COFOG) to both expenses and the net acquisition of nonfinancial assets.

COFOG classifies in detail the functions, or socioeconomic objectives, that general government units aim to achieve through kinds of outlays. COFOG permits analysts to examine over time the trends in government outlays on functions or purposes, regardless of the organizational structure of the government.

COFOG classifies objectives at three levels:

- At the highest level, COFOG identifies 10 divisions:
  1. General public services
  2. Defense
  3. Public order and safety
  4. Economic affairs
  5. Environmental protection
  6. Housing and community amenities
  7. Health
  8. Recreation, culture, and religion
  9. Education
  10. Social protection.
- It identifies within each division several groups.
- It identifies within each group one or more classes of activities, by which the broad objectives are achieved.

Counterparty Classification

The *GFSM 2001* also presents stocks of financial assets and liabilities and transactions in financial instruments by counterparty sector. This is to satisfy the interest of users in the sectors in which the government has outstanding claims/obligations and with which it is engaged in financial transactions. The economic classification classifies stock positions and transactions in financial assets and liabilities by types of financial instruments.

Resident counterpart sectors are the central bank, other depository corporations, financial corporations not elsewhere classified, nonfinancial corporations, households, and nonprofit institutions serving households (NPISH). Nonresident sectors are general government, international organizations, financial corporations, and other nonresidents.

VI

Linkages Among Macroeconomic Statistical Systems

International experts who designed the four main systems of macroeconomic statistics, described in the previous chapters, developed the systems to share many common features. Over the past two decades, the developers emphasized harmonization of the systems wherever possible, while maintaining the elements necessary in each specialized system to assist analysis. Although the specific needs of the specialized systems precluded full integration across systems, linkages across the systems reflect the many common features, promoting understanding and facilitating reconciliation to a large extent.

In addition, the high degree of harmonization allows integrating sectoral flows and stocks into macroeconomic analysis, as envisioned under the balance sheet approach (BSA). Finally, it substantially enhances data compilation, insofar as a single data collection effort can serve multiple uses.

The major harmonizations of the systems are in the following areas:

- *Residence.* All systems distinguish the domestic economy from the rest of the world on the same basis—residence of institutional units—assigning to the rest of the world those institutional units whose main center of economic interest is outside the geographic territory of the country.
- *Domestic economy and institutional sectors.* All systems define the domestic economy as all resident institutional units, adopting a common breakdown of the economy into sectors and subsectors.
- *Stocks and flows.* All systems use the same distinction between stocks—economic magnitudes measured at a point in time—and flows—economic magnitudes measured with regard to a period of time. Also, all systems use the same definitions for transactions and other economic flows.
- *Accounting rules.* All systems use the accrual basis for identifying and timing transactions. All systems use market prices as the valuation principle.

- *Boundary conditions.* For all systems,[38] the production and asset boundaries are the same.
- *Integrated accounts.* In all systems, an integrated set of accounts explains all changes between an opening and a closing balance sheet by transactions, holding gains/losses, and other changes in the volume of assets. This fosters analysts' ability to reconcile stocks and flows within balance sheets. In addition, the systems reflect harmonization in similar accounting frameworks, although substantial differences exist in classification to meet specific needs (Table 19).

For instance, *1993 SNA* focuses on measuring production and income flows in the current accounts—closely matched in the balance of payments. The *1993 SNA* rest-of-the-world account has identical coverage to the balance of payments but is presented from the point of view of the rest of the world, whereas the balance of payments presents the same data from the point of view of the reporting economy. The *1993 SNA* and balance of payments are the most completely harmonized of the systems.

In contrast, the government finance statistics (GFS) system uses quite different categories to meet the needs of fiscal analysis. This implies, for example, that the GFS do not include a production account and do not show the value of government final consumption expenditure.

As was noted in the relevant chapters, the monetary and financial statistics do not directly measure current account transactions. In the financial accounts, each system exhibits differences in classification, but these differences can be directly reconciled at the level of financial assets.

Readers can discern intersystem linkages, as they pertain to transactions, from the accounting frameworks presented side by side in Table 20.

The *1993 SNA* current accounts (Table 20, column 1) comprise the major aggregates and balancing items for the production and income accounts. In the current account, saving is the final balancing item. The parallel with the balance of payments framework (column 2) is evident because its current account includes the same components—goods and services, income, and current transfers—as the *1993 SNA* current accounts. This parallelism permits analysts to derive the links between *1993 SNA*. A

---

[38]The *Government Finance Statistics Manual 2001* (*GFSM 2001*; IMF, 2001) has one principal difference from the other systems, in that it recognizes that the government has an actual liability (and government employees have an asset) for government employee unfunded pensions.

TABLE 19. SCHEMATIC REPRESENTATION OF INTERSECTORAL LINKAGES

Real Sector

National accounts
Final consumption expenditure
  Government
  Other sectors
Capital formation
  Government
  Other sectors
Exports of goods and services
Imports of goods and services
Income and capital accounts
Net lending/borrowing
Financial account
  Net acquisition of financial assets
  Net incurrence of liabilities

External Sector

Balance of payments
Current account
  Exports of goods and services
  Imports of goods and services
  Net income
  Net current transfers
    Government
    Other sectors
Capital account
  Net capital transfers
    Government
    Other sectors
  Net acquisition of nonproduced, nonfinancial assets
Financial account
  Direct investment
  Portfolio investment
  Financial derivatives
  Other investment
  Reserve assets

Fiscal Sector

General government accounts
Revenue
Expense
Net operating balance

Net acquisition of nonfinancial assets

Transactions in financial assets and liabilities

Domestic financing
  Banks
  Nonbanks
External financing (net)

Monetary and Financial Sector

Depository corporations
Assets
  Net foreign assets
  Net domestic assets
    Net claims on central government
    Claims on other sectors
Liabilities
  Broad money
    Currency
    Transferable deposits
    Other deposits
    Securities other than shares
  Other liabilities
  Other items net

⟶ Accounting identities
┈┈▶ Strong accounting relationships

TABLE 20. COMPARISON OF MACROECONOMIC STATISTICAL SYSTEMS: TRANSACTION ACCOUNTS

System of National Accounts	Balance of Payments	Government Finance Statistics	Monetary and Financial Statistics[1]
Current account	*Current account*	*Transactions affecting net worth*	
Production account	Goods and services, credit	Revenue	
Output, basic prices	Goods: exports f.o.b.	Taxes	
– Intermediate consumption	Services	Social contributions	
= Gross, value added		Grants	
+ Taxes less subsidies on products	Goods and services, debit	Other revenue	
= GDP	Goods: imports f.o.b.		
	Services	Expense	
Generation of income account		Compensation of employees	
GDP		Use of goods and services	
– Compensation of employees		Consumption of fixed capital	
– Taxes less subsidies on production		Interest	
= Operating surplus/mixed income, gross		Subsidies	
	Income, credit	Grants	
Allocation of primary income account	Compensation of employees	Social benefits	
Operating surplus/mixed income, gross	Investment income	Other expense	
+ Compensation of employees			
+ Taxes less subsidies on production	Income, debit		
+ Property income, receivable	Compensation of employees		
– Property income, payable	Investment income		
= National income, gross			
	Current transfers, credit		
Secondary distribution of income account	Government		
National income, gross	Other sectors		
+ Current taxes on income, gross and wealth receivable			
– Current taxes on income and wealth payable			
+ Other current transfers, receivable			
– Other current transfers, payable			
= National disposable income, gross			

93

TABLE 20 (*CONCLUDED*)

System of National Accounts	Balance of Payments	Government Finance Statistics	Monetary and Financial Statistics[1]
Use of income account			
National disposable income, gross			
− Final consumption expenditure		Net operating balance	
= Saving, gross		= Revenue minus expenses[2]	
− Consumption of fixed capital	Balance on current account		
= Saving, net	= sum of all credit items above less sum of all debit items above[1]	Gross operating balance = Revenue minus expenses other than consumption of fixed capital	
			Transactions in nonfinancial assets
Capital account	*Capital account*	*Transactions in nonfinancial assets*	
Saving, gross	Capital transfers, credit	Net acquisition of nonfinancial assets	
+ Capital transfers, receivable	Government	Fixed assets	
− Capital transfers, payable	Other sectors	Change in inventories	
− Gross capital formation	Capital transfers, debit	Valuables	
− Acquisitions less disposals of nonproduced nonfinancial assets	Government	Nonproduced assets	
= Net lending (+)/net borrowing (−)	Other sectors		
	Nonproduced, nonfinancial assets, credit	Net lending/borrowing	
	Nonproduced, nonfinancial assets, debit	= Net operating balance minus net acquisition nonfinancial assets	
	Capital account balance = sum of credit items less sum of debit items		

Financial account	Financial account	Transactions in financial assets and liabilities	Financial account
Net acquisition of financial assets	Net transactions in financial assets[3]	Net acquisition of financial assets	Change in financial assets
Monetary gold and SDRs	Direct investment	Domestic	Net foreign assets
Currency and deposits	Portfolio investment	Foreign	Domestic claims
Securities other than shares	Financial derivatives		Net claims on central government
Loans	Other investment		Claims on other sectors
Shares and other equity	Reserve assets		
Insurance technical reserves			
Financial derivatives			
Other accounts receivable			
+ Net incurrence of liabilities	Net transactions in liabilities	Net incurrence of liabilities[5]	Changes in liabilities
Currency and deposits	Direct investment[4]	Domestic	Broad money
Securities other than shares	Portfolio investment	Foreign	Currency
Loans	Financial derivatives		Transferable deposits
Shares and other equity	Other investment		Other deposits
Insurance technical reserves			Securities other than shares
Financial derivatives			Other liabilities
Other accounts payable			Other items, net
	Financial account balance = sum of the above two items	Net acquisition of financial assets minus net incurrence of liabilities = Net lending/borrowing	
= Net lending (+)/net borrowing (−)			

[1]Presentation shown here relates to the depository corporations survey (DCS). For the financial corporations survey (FCS), see Chapter IV on monetary and financial statistics.

[2]Differs from "net saving" or "balance on current account" because capital transfers are included in revenue and expense.

[3]Includes some liability items.

[4]Includes some asset items.

[5]Differs from system of national accounts liabilities because of the inclusion in government finance statistics (GFS) of liabilities for government employees' pensions.

net saving and the balance of payments current account balance.[39] Table 21 shows a worked example illustrating some key *1993 SNA* and balance of payments links, based on data examples in the *1993 SNA*.

Users may derive this key linkage by focusing on the sources and uses of the total supply of goods and services in the economy. An economy can source total supply from domestic output (P) or imports (M). It can then be used in domestic production (intermediate consumption, IC); it can be consumed by households and NPISH (C); it can take the form of capital formation (I); it can be consumed by general government (G); or it can be exported (X). Thus,

Sources   Uses

$$P + M = IC + C + I + G + X. \tag{1}$$

Because GDP is output less intermediate consumption, users can restate the above identity as

$$GDP = C + I + G + (X - M). \tag{2}$$

This is the familiar GDP presentation by the *expenditure or final use method*.[40]

Gross national disposable income (GDY) equals GDP plus net primary income flows from abroad (NY) plus net current transfers from abroad (NCT):

$$GDY = C + I + G + (X - M) + NY + NCT, \tag{3}$$

and the current account balance (CAB) of the balance of payments is

$$CAB = X - M + NY + NCT. \tag{4}$$

So the gross national disposable income can be expressed as

$$GDY = C + I + G + CAB. \tag{5}$$

Given that saving (S) is gross national disposable income minus government and nongovernment consumption, then

$$S = GDY - C - G, \text{ or} \tag{6}$$

$$S = I + CAB, \text{ and} \tag{7}$$

$$S - I = CAB. \tag{8}$$

---

[39]The only difference between the *1993 SNA* and balance of payments current account classifications relates to financial intermediation services indirectly measured (FISIM). The *1993 SNA* allocates a portion of interest to imports and exports of services, whereas the balance of payments treats all interest as income; this has no impact on the current account balance.

[40]This equation is introduced in Chapter II.

TABLE 21. MAIN NATIONAL ACCOUNTS AGGREGATES FOR THE TOTAL ECONOMY (CONSOLIDATED) AND THEIR LINKS TO THE BALANCE OF PAYMENTS[1]

National Accounts (*1993 SNA*)		Balance of Payments	
Goods and services (consolidated)		*Current account*	
Gross domestic product (GDP)	**1,854**		
= Government final consumption expenditure (G)	368		
+ Nongovernment final consumption expenditure (C)	1,031		
+ Gross capital formation (I)	414	Goods and services	
+ Exports of goods and services (X)	540	Credit	540
– Imports of goods and services (I)	499	Debit	–499
		Total	51
Current and capital accounts (consolidated)			
GDP	**1,854**	+ Income	
+ Net primary income received from abroad (NY)	29	Credit	69
+ National income, gross	**1,883**	Debit	–40
+ Net current transfers received from abroad (NCT)	–29	Total	29
		+ Current transfers	
= National disposable income, gross (GDY)	**1,855**	Credit	10
		Debit	–39
– Final consumption expenditure (C + G)	1,399	Total	–29
		= Balance on current account (CAB)	41
= Saving, gross	**455**		
+ Net capital transfers received from abroad (NKT)	–3	*Capital account*	
		Credit	1
– Net acquisition of nonproduced, nonfinancial assets (NPNFA)	0	Debit	–4
		Total	–3
– Gross capital formation (I)	414		
= Net lending (+)/Net borrowing (–) (NL/B)	**38**		
Financial account		*Financial account*	
Net acquisition of financial assets less net incurrence of liabilities	38	Assets	–50
		less liabilities	88
= Net lending (+) Net borrowing (–)	38	Total	38

[1]In consolidated accounts, income and transfer flows among residents are not shown.

Thus, the balance of payments current account balance mirrors the saving and investment behavior of the whole economy. It equals the gap between saving and investment for the economy as a whole. If saving exceeds capital formation, the economy will have a current account surplus,

97

but if capital formation exceeds saving, the current account balance will be in deficit. Users can split both aggregates in equation (8) between government (g) and nongovernment (ng):

$$(S - I)g + (S - I)ng = (CAB)g + (CAB)ng. \tag{9}$$

If users drew a balance covering both the current and capital accounts of the balance of payments, then that balance would be identical to the net lending/borrowing balance for the whole economy of the national accounts. Saving minus investment plus net capital transfers (NKT) plus net acquisition of nonproduced, nonfinancial assets ($NPNFA$) defines the net lending/borrowing requirement (NL/B) for the economy as a whole:

$$NL/B = S - I + NKT + NPNFA, \text{ or} \tag{10}$$
$$NL/B = CAB + NKT + NPNFA. \tag{11}$$

Therefore, net lending/borrowing for the economy as a whole equals the total nonfinancial resources provided by the rest of the world. Disaggregating equation (10) into government and nongovernment provides a useful link to the GFS:

$$NL/B = NL/Bg + NL/Bng. \tag{12}$$

Users can align the *GFSM 2001* system with the *1993 SNA* and the current and capital accounts of the balance of payments, but some classification differences (described in detail in Box 16) prevent the full matching. The transactions that determine the GFS net operating balance (NOB) affect net worth and are divided into two categories—revenue (*REV*, that is, transactions that increase net worth) and expense (*EXP*, that is, transactions that decrease net worth). Whereas the major GFS categories do not reflect the *1993 SNA* breakdowns of current account transactions into production and income, the detailed GFS classifications permit users to closely reconcile outcomes between the two systems.

The *GFSM 2001* NOB differs from the *1993 SNA* net saving of the general government sector ($S - I)g$ mainly by the amount of net capital transfers received by government.

In any event, NL/Bg from equation (12) is a key link between the GFS and the *1993 SNA* and balance of payments:

$$NL/Bg = NOB + NANFA, \text{ where} \tag{13}$$
$$NOB = REV - EXP. \tag{14}$$

Users can directly link the GFS and balance of payments through the detailed classifications, because certain balance of payments standard components explicitly identify government transactions. These components include current transfers, capital transfers, portfolio investment, and other investment (see Chapter III on the balance of payments for descriptions). This also permits users to identify in the balance of payments the net acquisition of foreign assets and liabilities (*NAFAL*) that together with the net acquisition of domestic assets and liabilities (*NADAL*) constitute the financing of government operations. From equation (13) in the GFS,

$$NL/Bg = NAFAL + NADAL. \tag{15}$$

Regarding financing and the financial balance sheet, readers should recall that each statistical system specifically classifies financial assets and liabilities to meet its analytical needs. The *1993 SNA* classification of financial assets and liabilities follows the basic eight-category breakdown of financial assets and liabilities (see Box 2). The *1993 SNA* also supports the flow of funds, which, as described in some detail in the chapter on monetary and financial statistics, presents financial transactions by sector and type of financial asset. In its most comprehensive forms, the flow of funds is a detailed measure of which sectors and subsectors provide and receive financing and which type of financial asset they use in this financing.

As described in the chapter on balance of payments and international investment position (IIP), the balance of payments financial account and the IIP initially classify financial transactions into functional categories (direct investment, portfolio investment, other investment, financial derivatives, and reserve assets). The balance of payments and IIP coverage of financial assets and liabilities, however, is identical to the *1993 SNA*. And an asset and liability breakdown, very closely comparable with the *1993 SNA*, is available at the second level of the balance of payments classification, thus providing a strong link between the two systems. The balance of payments financial account also contains an abbreviated sectoral breakdown (monetary authorities, general government, banks, and other sectors) of the *1993 SNA* sectoral breakdown.

Turning to the monetary and financial statistics, readers should recall that, as described in the relevant chapter, the coverage of those statistics is limited to financial assets and liabilities,[41] corresponding to the *1993 SNA* financial account. Compiling data by financial instrument in all financial

---

[41]Except for transactions in nonfinancial assets of financial corporations, which are generally not of analytical significance.

surveys (that is, whether for central bank, depository corporations, or financial corporations) facilitates reconciling data with the *1993 SNA* financial account. Statistics covering depository corporations mainly focus on broad money liabilities (M), net foreign assets (NFA), and net domestic assets (NDA), with NDA comprising domestic credit (DC) and "other items, net" (OIN). Domestic credit is disaggregated into net bank credit to the government (NCG) and credit to other resident sectors ($CORS$):

$$M = NFA + DC - OIN, \text{ or} \tag{16}$$

$$M = NFA + NCG + CORS - OIN. \tag{17}$$

Changes in equation (17) can be represented by

$$\Delta M = \Delta NFA + \Delta NCG + \Delta CORS - \Delta OIN, \tag{18}$$

with Δ denoting period-to-period change.

Broader surveys of financial corporations also break down assets and liabilities by instrument, specifying whether nonresidents or the various resident subsectors hold these. Thus, the monetary and financial statistics are linked to the GFS by identifying claims on and liabilities to government units. National staff can compile data for claims on the central and general governments as well as other levels of government.[42]

A key link with the GFS can be expressed as:

$$NADAL = \Delta NCG + \Delta NCORS,[43] \tag{19}$$

where $\Delta NCORS$ is the change in net credit to government extended by other resident sectors.

The monetary and financial statistics are linked to the balance of payments through the identical residence criteria, detailed classifications, and comparable sectorization. The first order of classification in all financial surveys is to separate foreign and domestic positions and to compile data on nonresidents by type of financial asset and liability. Both systems allow compilers to measure positions of monetary authorities and banks (that is, depository corporations) held by the resident creditor for assets and the resident debtor for liabilities. Thus, users can readily identify, in the balance of payments, the NFA of the monetary authorities, as well as the NFA of the other financial corporations.

---

[42]The monetary and financial statistics can also separately identify claims on financial and nonfinancial public corporations, so credit provided to various definitions of the public sector can be measured provided that sectorization is sufficiently comprehensive.

[43]Net credit is taken to be identically equal to the net acquisition of financial assets.

In regard to *linkages across balance sheets*, the high degree of harmonization of the four statistical frameworks underpins the balance sheet approach (BSA) to macroeconomic analysis. Within the envelope of the *1993 SNA*, the balance sheets contemplated in the *MFSM*, the *GFSM 2001*, and the *BPM5* comprise the data on financial assets and liabilities, permitting analysts to identify cross-sectoral and cross-institutional claims. Indeed, analysts can assemble a comprehensive map of interresident and external financial obligations by suitable use of the balance sheets of the central bank, the depository corporations, the other financial corporations (all envisaged in the *MFSM*); the central and general governments (envisaged in the *GFSM 2001*); and the IIP (in the *BPM5*). Analysts can obtain this map, shown in Table 22, by organizing the balance sheets of the specified institutional units in matrix form—displaying in each specified block in the matrix the financial claims, liabilities, and net position of each institutional sector vis-à-vis the other specified institutional sectors.

Such a matrix of balance sheets—with adequate financial data breakdowns and complemented with data on nonfinancial assets—allows analysts to assess interinstitutional exposures and vulnerabilities. This assessment requires the analysts to disaggregate financial assets and liabilities by type of instrument, maturity (short-term, long-term), and currency (domestic, foreign) within the four statistical frameworks.[44]

In the matrix of balance sheets, analysts can organize each specified institutional block, subject to data availability, to show the subaggregates required for the relevant analysis. To comprehensively apply the BSA, however, analysts would need to complement the matrix with data on the value of nonfinancial assets. This is because the value of the nonfinancial assets in their balance sheets significantly determines the net worth position of the private subsectors. In particular, the counterparty to considerable financial obligations is the value of the holdings of residential and commercial property owned by the corporate and household subsectors.

---

[44]The existing macroeconomic systems do not fully address the disaggregations needed for the BSA, particularly the domestic/foreign currency breakdowns. However, the need for these extra details to facilitate vulnerability assessments has been addressed in the more recent work on external debt and public sector debt statistics (see chapter on balance of payments and international investment position and Box 18 on public sector debt).

TABLE 22. INTERSECTORAL ASSET AND LIABILITY POSITION MATRIX

Issuer of Liability (debtor) \\ Holder of Liability (creditor)	Central Bank	General Government	Financial Corporations	Nonfinancial Corporations and Other Resident Sectors	Nonresidents
Central bank Monetary base[1] Total other liabilities Short-term Domestic currency Foreign currency Long-term Domestic currency Foreign currency					
General government Total liabilities Short-term Domestic currency Foreign currency Long-term Domestic currency Foreign currency					
Financial corporations Total liabilities Short-term Domestic currency Foreign currency Long-term Domestic currency Foreign currency					
Nonfinancial corporations and other resident sectors Total liabilities Short-term Domestic currency Foreign currency Long-term Domestic currency Foreign currency					
Nonresidents Total liabilities Short-term Domestic currency Foreign currency Long-term Domestic currency Foreign currency					

[1]Refers to so-called high-powered money comprising central bank liabilities that support the expansion of broad money and credit.

Bibliography

Bank for International Settlements, Commonwealth Secretariat, Eurostat, International Monetary Fund, Organization for Economic Cooperation and Development, Paris Club Secretariat, United Nations Conference on Trade and Development, and World Bank, 2003, *External Debt Statistics: Guide for Compilers and Users* (Washington: International Monetary Fund).

Bloem, Adriaan M., Robert J. Dippelsman, and Nils Ø. Maehle, 2001, *Quarterly National Accounts Manual: Concepts, Data Sources, and Compilation* (Washington: International Monetary Fund).

Caves, Douglas W., Laurits R. Christensen, and W. Erwin Diewert, 1982, "The Economic Theory of Index Numbers and the Measurement of Input, Output, and Productivity," *Econometrica,* Vol. 50, No. 6 (November), pp. 1393–1414.

Commission of the European Communities—Eurostat, International Monetary Fund, Organization for Economic Cooperation and Development, United Nations, and World Bank, 1993, *System of National Accounts 1993* (Brussels/Luxembourg, New York, Paris, and Washington).

Diewert, W. Erwin, 1976, "Exact and Superlative Index Numbers," *Journal of Econometrics,* Vol. 4, No. 2 (May), pp. 115–45.

Galbis, Vicente, ed., 1991, *The IMF's Statistical Systems in Context of Revision of the United Nations' A System of National Accounts* (Washington: International Monetary Fund).

Høst-Madsen, Poul, 1979, *Macroeconomic Accounts: An Overview* (Washington: International Monetary Fund).

International Labor Organization, 2002, *Women and Men in the Informal Economy: A Statistical Picture* (Geneva). Available via the Internet: http://www.ilo.org/public/libdoc/ilo/2002/102B09_139_engl.pdf.

International Labor Organization, International Monetary Fund, Organization for Economic Cooperation and Development, Eurostat, United Nations Economic Commission for Europe, and World Bank, 2004a, *Producer Price Index Manual: Theory and Practice* (Geneva and Washington).

———, 2004b, *Consumer Price Index Manual: Theory and Practice* (Geneva and Washington).

International Monetary Fund, various issues, *International Financial Statistics* (Washington).

———, various issues, *Balance of Payments Statistics Yearbook* (Washington).

———, 1986, *A Manual on Government Finance Statistics* (Washington).

————, 1987, *Report on the World Current Account Discrepancy* (Washington).

————, 1992, *Report on the Measurement of International Capital Flows* (Washington).

————, 1993, *Balance of Payments Manual*, 5th ed. (Washington).

————, 1995, *Balance of Payments Compilation Guide* (Washington).

————, 1996a, *Balance of Payments Textbook* (Washington).

————, 1996b, *Coordinated Portfolio Investment Survey Guide* (Washington).

————, 1999, *Data Template on International Reserves and Foreign Currency Liquidity, Operational Guidelines, Provisional* (Washington).

————, 2000a, *Analysis of 1997 Coordinated Portfolio Investment Survey Results and Plans for the 2001 Survey* (Washington).

————, 2000b, *Financial Derivatives: A Supplement to the Fifth Edition (1993) of the Balance of Payments Manual* (Washington).

————, 2000c, *Monetary and Financial Statistics Manual* (Washington).

————, 2000d, *The New International Standards for the Statistical Measurement of Financial Derivatives: Changes to the Text of the 1993 SNA* (Washington). Available via the Internet: http://www.imf.org/external/np/sta/sna/2001/eng/changes/index.htm.

————, 2001, *Government Finance Statistics Manual* (Washington).

————, 2002a, *Coordinated Portfolio Investment Survey Guide*, 2nd ed. (Washington).

————, 2002b, *International Investment Position: A Guide to Data Sources* (Washington). Available via the Internet: http://www.imf.org/external/np/sta/iip/guide/index.htm.

————, 2003, *Data Quality Assessment Framework (DQAF)* (Washington). Available via the Internet: http://www.imf.org/external/np/sta/dsbb/2003/eng/dqaf.htm.

————, 2006, *Financial Soundness Indicators: Compilation Guide* (Washington).

————, 2007a, *The Special Data Dissemination Standard: Guide for Subscribers and Users* (Washington).

————, 2007b, *The General Data Dissemination System: Guide for Participants and Users* (Washington).

————, forthcoming, *Export and Import Price Index Manual: Theory and Practice* (Washington).

————, and the Organization for Economic Cooperation and Development, 2003, *Foreign Direct Investment Statistics: How Countries Measure FDI 2001* (Washington).

Kester, Anne Y., 2001, *International Reserves and Foreign Currency Liquidity: Guidelines for a Data Template* (Washington: International Monetary Fund).

Mathisen, Johan, and Anthony J. Pellechio, 2006, "Using the Balance Sheet Approach in Surveillance: Framework, Data Sources, and Data Availability," IMF Working Paper 06/100 (Washington: International Monetary Fund).

Organization for Economic Cooperation and Development, 1996, *OECD Benchmark Definition of Foreign Direct Investment*, 3rd ed. (Paris).

————, 2001, *Measuring Productivity: OECD Manual: Measurement of Aggregate and Industry-Level Productivity Growth* (Paris).

————, 2004, *Environmental Data Compendium 2004* (Paris).

————, International Monetary Fund, International Labor Organization, and the Interstate Statistical Committee of the Commonwealth of Independent States, 2002, *Measuring the Non-Observed Economy: A Handbook* (Paris). Available via the Internet: http://www.oecd.org/dataoecd/9/20/1963116.pdf.

Patterson, Neil, Marie Montanjees, John Motala, and Colleen Cardillo, 2004, *Foreign Direct Investment: Trends, Data Availability, Concepts, and Recording Practices* (Washington: International Monetary Fund).

United Nations, 1994, *Fundamental Principles of Official Statistics* (New York). Available via the Internet: http://unstats.un.org/unsd/goodprac/bpabout.asp.

————, 2000, *Household Accounting Experience in Concepts and Compilation: Vol. 1, Household Sector Accounts* (New York).

————, European Commission, International Monetary Fund, Organization for Economic Cooperation and Development, United Nations Conference on Trade and Development, and World Trade Organization, 2002, *Manual on Statistics of International Trade in Services* (Geneva, Brussels/Luxembourg, New York, Paris, Washington).

United Nations, European Commission, International Monetary Fund, Organization for Economic Cooperation and Development, and World Bank, 2003, *Handbook of National Accounting: Integrated Environmental and Economic Accounting 2003* (New York). Available via the Internet: http://unstats.un.org/unsd/envAccounting/seea2003.pdf.

United Nations Food and Agriculture Organization, 2004, *Integrated Environmental and Economic Accounting for Fisheries, Handbook of National Accounting*, Studies in Methods, Series F, No. 97 (New York). Available via the Internet: http://unstats.un.org/unsd/envAccounting/Fish_final_whitecover.pdf.